THE THIRTY YEARS PEACE

Translated from the German by
ROBERT AND RITA KIMBER

THE THIRTY YEARS PEACE

PETER O. CHOTJEWITZ

ALFRED A. KNOPF

NEW YORK 1981

THE THIRTY YEARS PEACE

1 Jürgen Schütrumpf is born on September 17, 1949, in N., a suburb of K.

When his parents meet in the spring of 1947, his father, Adolf Schütrumpf, has just been released from a POW camp and is taking night courses to prepare for his master plumber's exam.

He earns his money by working on his own in the plumbing and heating trade. This work is illegal because he has only apprenticed in this trade and does not yet have his master's license. He accepts silver, jewelry, rugs, and other valuables as payment and exchanges them on the black market for food produced in West Germany or pilfered from the occupying forces.

He frequents the Old Market of K. where the smugglers and fences have their quarters.

K. is in ruins. The center of the city is almost totally destroyed. So are the factories and public buildings. The areas on the edge of town and the suburbs have suffered less and in varying degrees. The bridges across the river are destroyed, too. A ferry that lands below the Old Market takes care of the traffic for the time being. Commercial life in the city is carried on at stands and sheds. In 1949, when the Federal Republic of Germany is to choose its capital, the citizens of K. quip that their town should be named capital of the Shederal Republic.

Edith and Adolf meet at the Old Market. Edith has time on her hands. Her mother and one of her brothers were killed in a bombing raid on K. Edith keeps house now and takes care of her father. His time as a prisoner of war has undermined his health so badly that he is dying. Edith is young and full of life. She has some contact with the black-market crowd, who can get hold of just about anything, and she knows a few theater people. Their favorite meeting place is a shed that calls itself the Gingerbread House Café.

In 1939, when Edith is sixteen, she dreams of becoming a dancer. One day she takes the trolley into town, finds the stage entrance to the theater on her first try, and confides in a handsome, graying stagehand whom she meets at the entrance and takes to be the director. He promises to get her a job in the chorus, deflowers her in the prop storeroom, and advises her not to become a dancer. Dancers get heavy thighs and muscular calves, he says. Besides, her breasts are too big.

Adolf appeals to the two main streaks in her character: a penchant for beauty and the higher things and a need to live in solid, predictable circumstances. Edith does not demand luxury, but she does want security.

She enjoys his sensitive and lengthy descriptions of the places he got to know during the war.

Through him, she comes to know Paris and Normandy without ever having been in either place, also Warsaw and the Vistula and the Vistula flounder that local fishermen grill over charcoal and sell on the riverbanks. Next come Prague, the Baltic, and, finally, Naples, Rome, and Florence.

After these adventures, he wound up in a POW camp near Kreuznach. The war was hard on him, but it provides her with further opportunity to admire him as he tells her about the art of survival he learned in the army. Others croaked in their foxholes because they had no self-discipline, because they ate up their rations right away, drank water that hadn't been boiled, and smoked all their cigarettes themselves instead of trading them for food.

Edith is impressed with Adolf. He manages to make the scraps of truth he has picked up look like the whole truth. He transforms the chemistry classes he is taking in plumbing school into a profound scientific study. When he stretches out on the grass and talks to Edith, Adolf is convinced that the superficial training in business methods that he and other budding tradesmen are getting from a denazified trade-school teacher will enable him to become the director of a major concern.

N. lies at the foot of a wooded range of hills. In the evening, the lovers often go out into the country and spread a blanket on the ground. Edith pulls up her skirt, and Adolf bares the natural wool of his athletic chest as he expounds on the mysterious interaction of the elements, explains physical laws, and even branches out into geology.

His talk excites Edith more than a few routine caresses on her body ever could. He subjugates her so effectively with words that she willingly gives herself to him when he is finally ready.

He asks her in French if she wants to sleep with him; tells her in Italian that he loves her; whispers Polish obscenities in her ear; and, when the evening mists reach the edge of the woods and he gets chilly, he says, "Let's go, Fräulein."

He is educated, can ask her in four languages if she wants a cigarette, and can sing the most popular opera arias from memory. Edith is particularly delighted with Adolf's artistic bent. She still loves operetta and light opera as much as she ever did. Puccini is her favorite. It works to Adolf's advantage that he did occasional stints as a stage technician in the early thirties when millions were out of work.

2   In the spring of 1949, Adolf Schütrumpf passes his master plumber's exam and sets up his own business in N. The black market has been in a decline for some time now, and Adolf is only one of many who are finding their way back into a normal working life. For Adolf, this change represents a step up the social ladder.

His father drove a beer truck for Kropf, and none of his brothers has his own business. Adolf thus adopts the principles of petty-bourgeois tradesmen at a time when this class is experiencing a regional renascence in the Federal Republic of Germany but, from a historical and worldwide perspective, has long since lost its significance in society.

Jürgen is already on the way when his parents marry, and Edith's father is still alive. He is on the verge of death and needs care more than ever, but the marriage takes precedence, especially since Edith's brothers Bübi and Bobo are no longer at home. Bobo, the older one, has been living in the north of town since the fall of 1948. His landlady, a widow by the name of Landgrebe, owns a beauty parlor. Bübi, the only member of the family ever to attend a *Gymnasium*, has just graduated at Easter and is beginning medical school in M. So Edith's father dies in a nursing home.

From the very beginning, Edith finds married life something of a strain and never fully adjusts to it. The summer of 1949 is hot, and she does not tolerate her pregnancy well. She has no great interest in housework, and though her efforts may have satisfied two younger brothers and a bedridden invalid, they are hardly adequate for a newly established tradesman in his thirties. Many of the stories Adolf tells in later years are comic episodes illustrating Edith's helplessness as a housewife. His listeners, including Edith herself, find these stories amusing, but it is also clear that Adolf tells them to expose an alleged incapacity on Edith's part to cope with the practical side of life.

For example, he tells how she roasted a duck once. When Adolf came home from work, he noticed a funny smell the moment he entered the kitchen. It turned out that Edith had browned the duck just as she should have and basted it regularly but had forgotten to draw it before she had put it in the oven.

Another time, she had neglected to hang out her wash and had left it standing in a tub. When Adolf eventually discovered the tub in a corner of the storeroom, some of the laundry was already moldy.

Until the day he dies, it is Adolf's feeling that Edith is incapable of managing money and property, even though she has been willing to learn from him.

Adolf takes the view that wives and housekeepers are made, not born. There are very few things a woman can do properly, if at all, without the right training from her husband. A marriage begins to show signs of success when a friend remarks someday to the husband: The little lady's coming along nicely, isn't she?

Edith comes along quite nicely under Adolf's strong hand, a hand that can also be tender and helpful.

3   Adolf is no pasha. He sees himself as the *paterfamilias*, as a father concerned for the welfare of his family. If his family defers to his infinite wisdom and well-intentioned advice, he rewards them with bread, beneficence, and love. He works to provide for his family. He knocks himself out for them. He gives his all. He expects no thanks, but he does assume that he, with his greater experience of life, will speak the last word in the family's affairs.

During the final weeks of Edith's pregnancy, he carries her up the stairs, straightens up the apartment after work, does the laundry, cooks for the next day, does the shopping. Even today, Edith enjoys recalling how Adolf waited on her hand and foot during her two pregnancies.

The memory of the birth itself spoils these otherwise pleasant recollections for her. As long as Jürgen can remember, she has referred to it as torture, but then she would usually hug him and say, "But you're my sweetheart all the same, aren't you?"

Jürgen will never rid himself of the guilt he feels for his difficult birth and for the fear of childbearing it inspired in his mother.

It takes almost three years before Adolf can get her pregnant again. If he had his way, they would have four sons and a daughter. He attributes Edith's unwillingness to have more children to pure self-indulgence and laziness. Since Jürgen remains the only child at this point, his parents concentrate their full attention on him.

They regard him as a prodigy; and, as they tell it, elderly ladies often peered into Jürgen's baby carriage and exclaimed: What a lovely child!

Later, when he learns to walk, he becomes the darling of the neighborhood and the nearby shopkeepers. One gives him a banana; another, a slice of wurst; still another, a piece of candy.

Jürgen learns how to talk early. His parents encourage him in this and show him off as something special.
"Say 'trolley car,' Jürgen."
"Lollytar."
"Elephant."
"Illifans."
"Stairs."
"Tares."

Because his parents use baby talk with him, his ability to speak improves very slowly. Patterns of speech developed within the family become institutionalized. When Jürgen is three, he is still asking, "Papa, nana eving at corner?"

As a reward, Adolf produces the banana he buys each evening at the corner grocery on his way home from work.

.   .   .

Jürgen is adept at imitating advertising blurbs, and he sings complete baby-talk versions of hit songs he hears on the radio. Edith finds this terribly cute, and she tries several times to get him onto a children's radio program.

Jürgen can do anything he likes, and all his desires are fulfilled. Bananas are his favorite food. He doesn't like wurst or any kind of vegetables. He won't eat bread or meat either. For years, Edith feeds him practically nothing but bananas and zwieback.

Late in the fall of 1952, Edith's second pregnancy is beginning to wear her down. Her interest in Jürgen drops off drastically. When he is three, she puts him in a nursery school where he is given lunch. To this very day, he recalls this time in the nursery school as the worst period of his life.

The teachers there pay little attention to his unusual dietary requests and try to make him give up his baby talk.

Up to this point, he is a typical only child without any playmates except for his mother, but it probably would still have been possible to integrate him into a group of children. However, the educational efforts of the nursery-school teachers stand in such sharp contrast to anything he has known before that he begins to withdraw. His tendency to isolate himself from others goes back to this period between his third and sixth year.

In January, 1953, Herbert is born. Edith's fear of childbirth complicates the delivery. She tenses up, suffers from shortness of breath during the birth, and goes into shock.

For Jürgen, his brother's birth means even further estrangement from his parents.

Adolf's attention is again focused on his wife. A man like Adolf finds self-realization in two ways: in his work and in procreation.

The birth of a second son gives him new strength. On the afternoon after the birth, he leaves the house to go visit his wife in the hospital.

He is all spruced up and wearing a light-colored suit.

He hears a tremendous racket on the street. A team of beer-wagon horses has shied and bolted. The driver is in the bar on the corner and has forgotten to put on the brake.

The wagon comes zigzagging headlong down the street, smashing into the cars parked on both sides of it. Out of control, the horses race toward the busy intersection of Frankfurter Strasse and Queralle.

Adolf drops his bouquet of flowers, runs out into the street, catches hold of the driver's seat, is dragged along for several yards, finally manages to climb up onto the seat, grab the reins, and brings the horses to a stop in time. He arrives at the hospital tattered and filthy. Edith is proud of him.

In the fall, Jürgen has an accident. While Edith is fixing Herbert's bottle, Jürgen climbs up on a chair next to her to watch. He slips and falls on the hard kitchen floor. He is not quite four at the time.

He has several bruises, some of them quite serious, but by far the worst injury he suffers is a skull fracture that continues to affect him for a long time. For years afterwards, he gets sick whenever he rides in a car, bus, or train. He also suffers from attacks of dizziness; and because his sense of balance is disturbed, he cannot turn around quickly, ride on swings, climb, or bend down.

4   The roles Jürgen's parents assume in their marriage during these years do not conform completely to the usual pattern. Adolf makes all the major purchases. Edith keeps house and cares for the children, but Adolf makes it his business to check on her work, too. Since he feels she cannot be trusted with money, he even does some of the food shopping, like buying their meat for the weekend.

In the butcher's shop, the meat is sold by a man. The women are allowed to sell only wurst, canned meats, and other such items. Adolf claims he has a better eye for meat and can deal with the butcher on an equal footing. This is why, in his opinion, he gets better cuts than Edith does.

Adolf also takes charge of buying household goods and clothing. Edith is allowed to express an opinion, but he always has the final say. If she buys a shirt, some underwear, or a tie without him, even as a birthday present, he thanks her but also expresses some criticism that proves he is a better shopper than she.

Adolf always cooks their Sunday dinner. When they gather mushrooms, Edith goes along but only to carry the basket. Adolf even bakes the cakes. Edith accepts all this without complaint. Adolf's impulse to do as much as possible himself, and his lack of faith in others' abilities, affects her more than anyone else, but these attitudes of his also feed into her tendency to take life easy and avoid responsibility. Only years later will she complain that Adolf treated her like a child from the earliest days of their marriage.

The children register their parents' behavior on a subconscious level, but in their minds, too, their father is the one who knows more about everything and can do things better, the one who is perfectly justified in wanting to do everything himself.

Jürgen's incapacity to deal with the major crisis of his life can be explained in part by the fact that he had no one at the time to tell him what to do. Still, his parents' marriage is not an unhappy one, and only toward the end of it does Edith begin to complain about her early years with Adolf.

The family spends most evenings at home. On summer evenings, Adolf usually works in the garden behind the house. Edith sits on a bench and looks up at the sky, which remains bright long after darkness has spread on the earth below it. The Schütrumpfs live in a six-family apartment house owned by a non-profit housing corporation. Four tenants keep small gardens behind the house.

Several evenings a week, Adolf dictates estimates and bills for Edith to type and talks over their business affairs with her. She keeps the books, prepares their tax returns, makes their social-security and health-insurance payments, submits bills to customers. By virtue of her training, she is more capable in this line than Adolf, and he recognizes this.

Once or twice a week, they go out to a movie, go bowling with friends, go to a carnival ball, sometimes to a musical. Once in a great while, they go to a concert of popular classics. On a few rare occasions in their lives, they stay up all night, drinking and dancing in a bar that has a telephone at every table—bars like this were very much the style in K. during the early fifties—and stopping for a nightcap at someone's apartment on the way home.

In reminiscing years later about these few evenings on the town, the Schütrumpfs and their friends manage to convince themselves that their youth was spent in stormy and riotous living. A man once invites Adolf and Edith and the couple with them to his table. He orders one bottle of champagne after another, buys liqueurs for the ladies, cigars for the men, and makes a great display of the bundle of hundred-mark notes in his wallet.

He orders a taxi and takes them all home to his house for a drink, puts on some music, opens up his well-stocked bar, turns the lights down low, whispers sweet nothings in the ladies' ears, and pats them playfully on rump and thigh. The plumber Schütrumpf and his friend, a house painter called Hassenpflug, begin to feel uneasy and suggest leaving since it is already morning and they have to be at work at seven.

All the same, this evening has a firm place in the Schütrumpfs' recollections of the good old days when they were first married. Stories like this always begin with the words "Do you remember the time when . . ."

The Schütrumpfs' sexual relationship is such that their day-to-day emotional life fluctuates like a sine whose curve gradually flattens out over the years. The sexually aggressive partner is the man. There are a number of ways in which he can express his desire for sex.

But there are only two answers: yes and no.

The brusqueness of her refusal annoys him, the way she pulls up her knees, turns her back to him, makes some remark about his appearance, his hair, his bad breath, his habit of rolling his eyes before he kisses her and losing control of his tongue.

The next morning, Father is irritable. His workers joke about it among themselves.

"Boy, is he in a rotten mood today. I bet his old lady didn't let him get in last night."

Edith refuses him a lot without exactly knowing why. He makes her pay for it, growls at her, is pickier than ever. His criticism doesn't bother her. She doesn't realize until quite late in their lives that her refusal was a way of getting back at him for his patriarchal tyranny, a kind of rebelling against his impenetrable self-esteem.

If Edith gives in, Adolf is more helpful and pleasant than usual the next day. Edith knows that. She strikes a balance between rejection and acceptance that keeps their marriage from foundering. Adolf realizes this, too. He loves his wife. For him, love consists of giving and taking. He rewards affection with affection, rejection with rejection. A marriage without sex would be as inconceivable for him as a life without marriage would be for Edith.

On some unconscious level, they settle into a marriage that is reasonably happy over extended periods of time. As the sine curve flattens out more and more, the drama and tension of the marriage relationship fade. What remains is a routine and somewhat tired life in harness. Feeling gives way to petty haggling. In marriages like this, what both partners hope for, without knowing it, is the early death of the other.

5   None of this is evident in family snapshots taken in the mid-fifties. One picture shows Edith as a shapely dark-haired woman with a permanent. She is quite stylishly dressed and wears a fox stole over her shoulders. In another picture, supposedly taken at about the same time, Adolf is wearing a stiff, light-colored hat and an elegant double-breasted, dark blue overcoat. The crease in his pants is razor sharp. He has one glove on and carries the other in his gloved hand, as was the fashion at that time. He is dressed to kill.

Another picture shows Edith in one of those see-through blouses that were in style then, but with a bra and slip under it, of course. Adolf is in his shirt-sleeves but has on a tie. They are sitting at a table at a party and looking lovingly at each other. Adolf's thin hair is damp and combed straight back. An attractive couple.

Jürgen is a pretty child with curly blond hair. He looks delicate in his appropriately cute clothes as he sits squeezed between his parents, who are perched stiffly on a park bench. A fancy baby carriage, no doubt with little Herbert in it, stands next to them. Edith's hand rests on the handlebar.

Jürgen does not hear about his parents' occasional nocturnal adventures until he is out of school. In his memories of childhood, he has an image of his mother looking like an elegantly dressed lady in a magazine as she leans over his bed to kiss him good night before she goes out with Adolf. She smells good, and her kiss tastes of lipstick. He still remembers that clearly.

Adolf has one or two other men working with him, sometimes even three during his busiest season, and he also has an apprentice until well into the sixties. He puts in a full day on the job himself and does his calling on customers in the evenings. His workday usually runs from seven in the morning until five-thirty or six in the evening. Then he has to take care of whatever paperwork Edith does not handle.

.   .   .

Edith has no real interest in the business.

His friends often urge him to expand so that he can take on larger jobs in construction work. Adolf is leery of making such a large investment. He would have to go into debt for a while, and he doesn't like that idea at all. He's afraid, too, that his workers will slack off if he isn't there to keep an eye on them every minute.

He's satisfied with what he has: a three-room apartment in a housing project; a rented workshop a block away from Frankfurter Strasse, which goes right through the center of N.; since 1955 even a car. The first one is a Lloyd Alexander. After that, he has Fords. Adolf always drives station wagons. Edith is not altogether pleased with them and would prefer a regular sedan.

But the Schütrumpfs still have financial worries even though Adolf's income is large enough to cover their expenses and he earns more as an independent tradesman than a plumber working for someone else can. Adolf, who claims that Edith can't handle money, can't handle it himself. Money seems to slip through their fingers, and neither of them knows exactly where it has gone.

This makes Adolf more suspicious than ever. He doles out household money to Edith and makes her account for every last penny of it. He establishes special funds for all kinds of expenditures, stashing the money away in innumerable cigar boxes. He feels that his friends and relatives exploit him, that his customers and workers get the best of him, that salesmen and suppliers cheat him.

Things soon get so bad that the Schütrumpfs resent getting a gift because they feel it forces them to respond in kind. They accept fewer and fewer invitations so that they won't have to extend any. Old friendships die out before the Schütrumpfs are even aware of it. Adolf complains that there are hardly any nice people left anymore. Edith agrees with him, but her voice lacks conviction.

After ten years of marriage, Adolf and Edith have very few friends left. They have lost touch with their relatives, even with their own brothers and sisters. They rarely go out at all anymore. They have gradually succumbed to pettiness and isolation. Edith is not allowed to take the trolley to K. She has to walk the three kilometers, and she pretends that she does this of her own accord. Most of the Schütrumpfs' marital disagreements are about money.

6 Jürgen starts school in the fall of 1955, just before his sixth birthday. He is a small child, delicate, nervous, and pale. Edith is looking forward to a little more time for herself. Jürgen will go to an after-school program where he will eat his midday meal and stay until four o'clock.

Adolf is all for sending Jürgen to school, because it's never too early to enter the mainstream of life and begin acquiring experience. Adolf's own educational methods resemble alternate hot and cold baths. At one time, he is helpful, loving, and affectionate with his children. At another, he is hard on them, demands too much of them, and leaves them to their own devices when they most need his help.

Jürgen's teachers describe him as an interested and lively pupil. He is quick to learn. He is having some difficulty expressing himself orally, but in the first years of school this is no great problem. The most striking thing about him is his tendency to show off. He often plays the clown and disrupts the class if he feels he can win the applause of his schoolmates by doing so.

His teachers think he behaves this way to make up for the fact that he is one of the smallest children in his class and is not permitted to take gym with the others.

He has difficulty making friends, feels isolated, and thinks the other children are making fun of him and consider him not quite normal.

Whenever he is put on the spot, he feels an irrepressible urge to move his bowels. In his first years at school, he often comes home with soiled underwear or with his pants full. He has inherited this from Edith. She often has to run to the toilet when Adolf is determined to have a heart-to-heart talk with her. He interprets this as rebelliousness and a lack of interest in what he has to say, and he bawls her out for it. After several years of this, the very thought that he might forbid her to go to the bathroom is enough to prompt a bowel movement.

Jürgen is reluctant to use the school toilets. He gets this from Adolf, who has an aversion for public toilets. Adolf is also wary of accepting food from strangers. Once when the Schütrumpfs stop for a drink at the Gasthaus zur Mitte, the restaurant and bar in the center of N., Jürgen says he is hungry. Adolf orders him a bowl of chicken soup with egg in it. The waiter brings the soup but forgets the spoon.

A man at a neighboring table offers Jürgen a spoon. Adolf knocks it out of the man's hand. Jürgen is upset by this, but the thing that bothers him most is how hurt the man must feel. When they get home, Adolf explains that there is no way of knowing whether the man had already used the spoon or not.

Jürgen has no friends and only occasional playmates until he is twelve. For a while, Jürgen plays with a boy his age who lives on the second floor of their apartment house. But Adolf doesn't like the boy's family. The father works in a beauty parlor. Adolf just doesn't cotton to that type. The man strikes him as a bit of a sneak. Besides, Adolf thinks that anybody who's a hairdresser has homosexual tendencies.

A few months after the family moves in, the boy dies of a heart disorder.

Jürgen is invited to other children's birthday parties a few times, but Adolf and Edith spoil these parties for him with their derogatory remarks. What they are really afraid of is having to give a children's party themselves, and they resent having to spend money on birthday presents.

When Herbert is four, he goes to kindergarten, and Jürgen can come home directly now instead of going to his after-school program. He and his mother become closer again. If we can believe what she says, she feels that Jürgen needs someone he can turn to and pour his heart out to.

That is probably only half the truth. Edith has always unconsciously served her own interests by ostensibly serving those of others. The farther she withdraws from Adolf, the greater her affection for Jürgen becomes. By paying a lot of attention to Jürgen she makes her husband jealous. He accuses her of neglecting him, the housework, and her part of the business. This allows her in turn to accuse him of selfishness, neglect of the children, and constant nagging. These discussions do not alleviate the impending crisis in their marriage but instead aggravate it.

Edith often lets Jürgen sleep in her bed. Adolf sees this as an infringement on his sacred and exclusive territory. She continues to bathe Jürgen, even washing his genitals for him, until he is fourteen.

There is a kernel of truth in her explanation for her behavior. Edith senses that Jürgen's insecurity and inhibitions are partially the result of his father's overbearing nature. From their earliest childhood, Adolf has let his sons feel their inferiority and their dependence on him.

Adolf does not realize that his wife and son are rebelling against him. He makes fun of her excessive display of maternal love, accuses her of coddling the boy, and derides Jürgen's lack of robustness.

7   Herbert takes more after his father. He vacillates between a need to submit and a need to dominate, between rowdiness and gentleness, aggressiveness and affection, generosity and vindictiveness, euphoria and depression. Edith and Jürgen live in a minor key, experiencing nothing in excess, neither pain nor pleasure. Even on those few occasions when they do something unusual, their actions seem to have something accidental and unobtrusive about them. They would make ideal criminals. No one would suspect them of anything.

. . .

Given the proper circumstances, Adolf and Herbert are capable of anything. They can become blind with fury. Depending on which side of Herbert's nature happens to predominate at any particular moment, he and his father will love or hate each other.

Whenever Herbert enrages his father, Adolf claims that the boy is clearly a bastard, not his son at all, some kind of freak.

For almost twenty years, Jürgen and Herbert have little more in common than the same parents and the parents' values, which each son absorbs in a different way. They are exposed to the same social milieu, the same principles, and the same circumstances. Even their schooling and vocational training follow similar paths. In spite of this, they develop quite differently. Only later will Herbert get closer to his brother, sympathize with him, and try to understand him.

8 At ten, Jürgen is sent to *Realschule*, a secondary school designed for students who will not go on to the university. His teachers in elementary school recommend that he go to the *Gymnasium*. Edith, who opens the letter from the school, is sure that Adolf will agree to this. The first thing Adolf does when he comes home is to eat supper. He doesn't want to be bothered during the meal.

After supper, Edith shows him the letter. His eyes flash with feigned indignation. Why didn't you show me this letter right away? It's clear that he is much more proud than angry. His son! Jürgen is pleased that he will be going to the *Gymnasium*. The children in elementary school are too crude for his tastes.

This is the age when children start using dirty language. This language is painful to Jürgen, but he uses it anyhow so that he won't call attention to himself. Halfheartedly but with a great deal of outward bravado, Jürgen uses a lot of words whose meanings are not quite clear to him. He says "muck" instead of "fuck." The other kids laugh at him. Ha-ha, Jurgen doesn't know what fucking is.

Sometimes he reads or hears words he thinks are dirty. Like the word "biceps." He thinks that's another word for penis. There's a boy in the eighth grade who already looks like a man. The fourth-graders are hanging around the door of the boys' room, the way they often do.

"I bet he's got a huge biceps," Jürgen puts in casually. The others simply ignore his remark as they always do when they don't understand something.

Jürgen is disappointed. He was expecting admiration. For once, he has come up with a new word.

After a few weeks, his interest in obscene language has given way to aversion. He gets into an argument. At recess, the boys are talking about adult sex. They all claim to have seen older people having intercourse. Older people means anybody over fourteen.

Jürgen says that when he thinks about this period now it strikes him as amusing, sometimes even as downright funny. The stories the other boys told then excited him. One of them told about standing in a back courtyard once. A newly married couple had just moved into a fourth-floor apartment, and the boy had seen an older couple go up the stairs together with the younger pair.

After a while, the older couple came down into the courtyard and walked up and down between the bushes and flower beds. A little while later, the young man leaned out of the window and called to them, "You can come up again."

All he had on above the waist was his undershirt.

The boys are convinced that the young couple went to bed together. That's why the parents came down to the courtyard. Jürgen does not dispute this, but he claims that his parents haven't had any sex together since they conceived their children. The other boys laugh at him.

Jürgen's world is shattered. If the other boys are right, then at every minute of the day everywhere in the world people are copulating by the millions.

He finds the girls particularly exciting. They're always huddling together, clucking and giggling and nudging each other whenever a boy comes around. Jürgen is convinced that they want him to grab them, possibly even fuck them. He's heard that a few boys and girls in his class are already having sexual relations.

The older boys in the school brag to the younger ones about their sexual experiences. A fourteen-year-old tells Jürgen about his cousin who is the same age as he is. She often comes with her parents to visit. A while after the guests arrive, the adults send the boy and his cousin off to play in the children's room. Then he takes her into the bathroom, and they do it together.

This is the age when children begin to imitate adult sexual roles and attitudes. If a girl makes fun of a boy, the boys say, "What she needs is a good fucking."

In the boys' view, the purpose of sexual intercourse is to show the girls who's boss and knock the freshness out of them.

The boys are fascinated by pictures of nudes and by books with pornographic passages in them. In these books, a woman is not really a woman until she has lost her virginity and had a good screwing.

Jürgen feels increasingly repelled by his schoolmates' dirty jokes and constant references to sex. He finds it impossible to hang around with girls, feel them up, whisper propositions to them. Once, as he is walking past a girl, he smacks her on the rump with the flat of his hand.

The blood rushes to his head, he feels hot, his legs go wobbly under him, his stomach churns, everything goes blurry before his eyes.

And at the same time he has the feeling that his gesture has wakened an interest in the girl, which frightens him. He fears the girl will react by making sexual demands on him. Whenever he sees the girl, he tries to avoid her.

·　　·　　·

At the *Gymnasium*, everything will be different, he hopes. The students there have better manners and are not as vulgar as they are in the elementary school. In his neighborhood, there are several children who go to the *Gymnasium*. They all come from better families, a fact that Adolf and Edith readily acknowledge.

9   Adolf's decision not to send Jürgen to the *Gymnasium* is typical of the lower middle class and the working class. Girls are at an even greater disadvantage than boys. They'll all get married anyhow, and you don't need any great education for that. Their parents largely determine what occupations they will take up. Women's jobs—kindergarten teacher, secretary, post office clerk, and so on—don't require advanced schooling. Most children from this kind of background accept their parents' decisions about their future under the illusion that they have made a decision for themselves.

Adolf feels that Jürgen should not spend the rest of his life in school. Academic careers are all right for children who come from families with academic training, but children of Jürgen's background should not set their sights too high. Adolf's aversion for anything intellectual or out of the ordinary is paradoxically coupled with respect for certain academic professions, like law and medicine. He considers intellectuals models as long as they are conservative and class-conscious, as long as they uphold established standards of style and etiquette. This presupposes the kind of breeding that can only be had in a good family. It's a pleasure to know people like that.

The Schütrumpfs are, of course, a good family. A skilled craftsman will always have work. Nobody can look down on a man with a master's license in his trade, and nobody is any better off than an independent tradesman. But in spite of all this, Adolf betrays a prejudice against his own class. He tells about a boy who had his heart set on going to the university. He studied so hard that he had a nervous breakdown. According to Adolf, intellectual and artistic work leads to madness. Another young man couldn't stand the social pressure. He lived in constant fear that people would notice from his behavior that he came from a poor family.

Adolf's main arguments are economic ones. By the time the others have finished at the *Gymnasium*, you'll have your training behind you and be making good money; and while the others are still studying at the university, you'll have your master's license and maybe even your own business. You'll be way ahead of them in practical experience. Not to mention the money you'll be earning.

Jürgen goes to *Realschule*. There's always the possibility that he can transfer to the *Gymnasium* later. For a few days, he cries at night before he goes to sleep. In his fantasies, the girls who go to the *Gymnasium* take piano lessons. Some of them take riding lessons, too. The boys have huge electric train sets, a microscope, a chemistry set they use to perform experiments with, a Ping-Pong table on the porch, and a big dog to play with. In the summer they go away with their families on vacation. Some of them have maids.

Adolf is responsible for these fantasies. Between N. and the long wooded ridge above K. there is a large suburb called Kuhberg, with nothing but villas, mansions, and ranch houses in it. Adolf has customers in Kuhberg and describes how people live there. He doesn't approve of that kind of luxury. Edith isn't so sure. She wouldn't mind a little more than they have. I would have liked a fur coat, she says. She has one now.

Jürgen seems to have made his peace with his father's decision. He accepts it the same way that he accepts Adolf's choice of profession for him a few years later. Apparently there is no conflict between father and son. Today, Jürgen is practically obsessed with the thought that the wrong choice of schooling and trade set his whole development off on the wrong footing.

1 0   At twelve, Jürgen begins to masturbate. He spends a lot of time with a boy named Pels, who is almost two years older and attends the *Gymnasium*. One evening, Pels suggests that they masturbate together. Jürgen doesn't know how to do it. It is late fall. Jürgen remembers the scene vividly. They are in a lonely corner of the city park.

Pels says: Come on, I'll show you how. He leans back on his elbows with his large penis sticking straight up out of his fly.

Give me your hand.

Jürgen wraps his fingers around his friend's penis and begins to masturbate him awkwardly.

Pels thrusts with his hips. Faster, he says, faster. After a while Jürgen gets a cramp in his hand. I can't do it anymore, he says, and he lets go. Pels takes hold himself and moves his hand up and down with incredible speed. When he comes, he makes horrible faces and twitches all over. Jürgen is impressed.

This brings up another memory. It is Sunday noon. He is supposed to tell his father to come home for the midday meal; the men are having a glass of wine at the Gasthaus zur Mitte

Dr. Frütrunk, the Schütrumpfs' dentist, who lives on Heckelstrasse, is shaking with laughter and exclaiming: The first time I came, I thought my spinal cord was leaking out!

A few days later, Pels takes Jürgen into a side path in the park that is thickly lined with shrubbery. Pels stops, pulls out his penis, and starts to masturbate. He encourages Jürgen to do the same. Jürgen tries but manages only a few strokes. The feelings of pleasure are unbearable and in some strange way almost painful.

A few days after that, he is riding his bicycle to a village outside K. to visit his father on the job and bring him his breakfast. While riding on the deserted country road, he pulls out his penis and tries again to masturbate. It goes better this time, but the indescribable feelings of pleasure once again prevent him from masturbating to orgasm. He has still not experienced ejaculation.

From the very beginning, Jürgen thinks masturbation is a kind of original sin. It's not that he is ashamed, but he feels he has entered a new and degraded phase of his life. He has a sense of loss. When he thinks back on his youth, he divides it into the period before he began masturbating and the period after.

Adolf issues warnings to his sons. Without looking directly at them, he talks about the dangers of masturbation. He points out small, pale, sickly boys and says they got that way from masturbating. He tells about seeing an adolescent standing around in front of the movie house with his hand in his pants pocket, playing with his penis. Everybody looked at him with disgust, but the boy was oblivious to them.

Adolf represents masturbation as a dangerous addiction that debilitates those afflicted with it and forces them to play with themselves all the time. If you once start, you end up having to masturbate five or six times a day. Masturbation not only robs you of your physical strength but also affects your mind.

The minister whose confirmation classes Jürgen attends in the spring of 1961 frequently sends the girls home early and lectures the boys on the dangers of masturbation. If a married man comes and complains that he has had a fight with his wife, the first question the minister asks is whether the man masturbated the night before. He recommends that the boys eat apples and drink cold water whenever they feel the urge to masturbate. If that doesn't work, a two- or three-mile run may help.

1 1 For years, Pels is Jürgen's only friend. Jürgen remembers the first time he became aware of sexual feelings for Pels. Pels picked him up at his house. He had his bicycle with him. Pels sat on the back of the seat and had Jürgen sit in front of him. As they rode together, Jürgen could feel Pels's penis against his buttocks.

Pels was proud of his penis. It was fully developed, considerably larger than Jürgen's, and always half erect. Pels's penis played an important role in their relationship. They called it "Bimbo." When Pels rode his bicycle next to Jürgen, Jürgen would say: Let's ride Bimbo. Pels would nod, and Jürgen would climb on the bike with him.

Jürgen doesn't realize that Pels is exploiting him sexually. For about two years between Jürgen's twelfth and fourteenth year, they go up to the Schütrumpfs' attic three or four times every month. There is an old sofa up there. Jürgen takes off his pants and lies down on his back. Pels sticks his erect penis between Jürgen's thighs. Jürgen squeezes his legs together, and Pels moves his hips up and down rhythmically until he has an orgasm. After a few weeks the sofa is covered with stains.

Jürgen never has an orgasm on these occasions, never asks Pels to masturbate him, and, with the exception of the first two unsuccessful attempts, he never masturbates in Pels's presence. He tells Pels he never masturbates and acts surprised at his friend's strong sexual urge. He claims he does not have such needs.

Adolf disapproves of this friendship with Pels from the very beginning. He says Pels is a bad influence on Jürgen. He especially dislikes Pels's parents. They strike Adolf as pretentious, even though they are worse off than the Schütrumpfs. Pels's father runs a paint store on Frankfurter Strasse, and Frau Pels gives piano lessons for beginners.

.   .   .   .

Jürgen still sees these years with Pels as the happiest of his life. He and Pels understand each other almost intuitively. Sometimes they meet on the way to each other's house because they have both felt an impulse, at the same time, to tell the other something. Then they discover they have had the same thought or done the same thing.

Edith admits that she and Adolf worried about Jürgen during this time. His friendship with Pels was so close that she sometimes felt she could not get through to him. The two boys lived in a world of their own.

1 2   When Jürgen is fourteen, the sexual contact with Pels comes to an end. Their friendship continues as though nothing had changed. Jürgen convinces a boy from the house next door to go up to the attic with him a few times. He tries to do what Pels did with him, but the boy's bony legs offer no firm hold for his small penis. After the third time, the boy refuses to go to the attic again.

Pels is pursuing the older sister of a boy named Uwe Hühnerfuss, whose family also lives in N. Several years later, Jürgen and Hühnerfuss become friends for a while.

One morning on the way to school, Pels, with an air of mystery, raises a finger in the air, sniffs at it frequently, and tries to stir Jürgen's curiosity. Jürgen can't smell anything. Pels says he hasn't washed that finger for three days because he didn't want to wash off the girl's smell.

Pels's claim that he stuck his finger into the girl comes as a surprise to Jürgen and hurts him. He is envious. Since he has no prospects of similar adventures, he feels that Pels should not indulge in them either.

This envy remains a basic component in Jürgen's nature even now, and even though he has become aware of it in himself. He feels that no one else should be able to own, experience, achieve, or do more than he can. He knows, of course, that this is an unrealistic expectation, but he secretly reproaches anyone who seems to surpass him in any way.

For years, his attempts to approach girls end in failure. He gawks at a girl for a long time, follows her around, thinks what he will say to her, but never works up the courage to actually speak to her.

Then at some point he gives up the pursuit. Now he is angry with himself for failing again. To make himself feel better, he invents all kinds of excuses. The whole thing was pointless anyhow, the girl wasn't his type, and so on. If a girl shows signs of welcoming his overtures, he turns away abruptly and goes.

He tells a story from his school days.

One of the events at a class party when he is in the eighth grade is a beauty contest. The boys dress up as girls and the girls as boys. Then the boys pick the girl they think is the handsomest man in the class and vice versa.

Jürgen works on his costume and makeup for days ahead and gets a flaming red wig. He is elected beauty queen. The girls admire him, run their hands over him, touch his dress, caress his hair, kiss him, and swarm all over him. He has to lift up his skirt and show his legs.

The girls' behavior does not embarrass him, and he doesn't mind being close to them as long as he is wearing girls' clothes. Later, the boys choose their beauty queen from among the girls. Then there is a raffle. The prize for the three winners is a kiss from the girl judged "most handsome." Jürgen wins first place in the raffle.

Once the excitement has died down and the prize is about to be awarded, Jürgen is nowhere to be found. The whole class sets out to find him, and he is discovered in the bathroom. The janitor has to be summoned to unlock the door. Then Jürgen's classmates drag him back to their homeroom. He is pale as a sheet and feels sick to his stomach. He blacks out as he nears the front of the room, and when the others let go of him he falls flat on the floor in front of the girl.

. . .

The winner of the second prize is shy, too, but he gets hold of himself and lets himself be kissed on the cheek. The third winner struts like a bullfighter, marches boldly to the front, and receives his kiss, posing like a film star whom all the women are just dying to kiss.

Jürgen recalls that class party as one of the most humiliating experiences of his life.

1 3 Ten years later, Jürgen is able, in the course of a conversation, to analyze the reasons for his difficulties with girls at that time.

Jürgen's interest in girls is exclusively sexual. He wants to relate to them the way Pels and the other boys do, telling about their sexual adventures afterwards. In doing this, they are merely following in the footsteps of their fathers' generation.

Jürgen sometimes visits his father on the job and stays for a while. Sometimes the workers from several firms sit together at their coffee break. Sex is one of the main topics of conversation.

An older married man tells how he had sex with his wife several times the night before. The first time he went in from in front. Then he said: Okay, now the other way round. Jürgen tells this story to Pels.

The expression "Okay, now the other way round" becomes a set phrase for the two boys and a code word for sexual adventure.

Jürgen feels some doubt about the veracity of the stories he hears. He pictures the older married man and his wife in their underwear and imagines them having intercourse. The image he conjures up does not correspond to his notion of sexual delight.

He has trouble believing, too, judging from the many married couples he knows, that sex plays any significant role in their marriages. And he is both obsessed and repelled by all this fuckity-fuck stuff, as he has come to call it in his mind.

Jürgen visits an old friend, a cabinetmaker who lives on a side street off Frankfurter Strasse. Jürgen sometimes watches him at his work,

and he thinks that if he has to choose a trade at sixteen, he would like
to be cabinetmaker and have his own small shop.

One day he asks the old man if adults really think about fucking all
the time and fuck as much as they claim. The cabinetmaker shakes
his head and says, "By the time you're forty or fifty, there's not much
doing at home. That's all a lot of stupid talk."

This answer only partially placates him. The workers may exag-
gerate, but there is something real about their desires, and what they
say makes Jürgen more eager than ever to sleep with a girl.

Nobody discusses with him what a relationship between a man and a
woman might be like and what it needs to be meaningful.

The idealized descriptions of married love in the books Edith
devours are of no use to him either.

He can't make contact with a girl because he does not see her
primarily as a person. All he does see in her is a pair of breasts and a
triangle between her thighs. He sometimes thinks that all women
should be forbidden to wear underwear; and whenever a man or boy
asked, they would have to have sex with him. That would be the
solution. A man could just help himself the way he does at a cigarette
machine.

In 1963, when the newspapers are playing up the threat of another
world war, Jürgen is not the least bit upset. He has heard that
standards of sexual morality declined during the last war. During
wartime, he thinks, the girls are more willing. Nor is he afraid of the
Russians. He hopes that the Communists will institute free love. His
friends are flabbergasted. What an idiot, they say.

On winter evenings, he walks the streets and looks into lighted
windows. If he sees a woman, he stops, hoping she'll take her clothes
off. If a man comes into the room, he hopes the couple will make love
with the light on. Sometimes he sees a woman take off her sweater,
but then, perhaps sensing that someone is watching her, she leaves
the room or turns the light out. In two or three winters of this, Jürgen

never gets to see a naked woman, let alone a couple having intercourse.

Before going to sleep he masturbates like crazy. He uses condoms he takes from the drawer in his father's bedside table so he won't stain the sheets. What the hell keeps happening to my rubbers? he hears his father complain. The idea that his parents have sex together drives him frantic with excitement. Adolf suspects his wife of throwing the condoms out so that she won't have to sleep with him.

When he masturbates, Jürgen fantasizes about the breasts he has seen during the day. For weeks on end his masturbation fantasies dwell on the immense breasts of the woman in the first-floor apartment. She is about forty. He masturbates during the day, too. Whenever he sees a young girl who is just beginning to get breasts or a woman whose breasts appeal to him, he runs for the closest bathroom.

Masturbation gives him no satisfaction. It is a poor substitute that constantly reminds him he is incapable of forming a relationship with a girl.

1 4 Girls his own age excite him the most. They wear tight sweaters and are obviously proud of their breasts. At school they catch hold of each others' bras in back and snap the elastic. Some of them stuff handkerchiefs into the breast pockets of their blouses and jackets to make their breasts look bigger.

There is a girl he thinks he can trust. One day he says to her: Will you come to our garden shed this evening? She agrees. At dusk he drags an old mattress into the shed and waits for her for hours. He comes into the house chilled to the bone. His parents bawl him out.

In the summer of 1965, shortly before he becomes sixteen, he has a girl friend for the first time. He spends hours hanging around her house. If she happens to come out, he pretends he is there just by chance. Do you want to go to the park with me?

He trots along next to her like an idiot, tries to make conversation, doesn't know what he should do with her. He wonders if he should ask if he can kiss her, then finally does ask: Would you like to sit down?

This goes on all summer long, two or three times each week.

Adolf keeps an eye on his sons, first Jürgen, then Herbert. He shadows them, hides in the bushes when they sit on a park bench with their girls. He once gets tangled in the brush and falls down. Jürgen and his girl are startled. Adolf manages to get away without being recognized.

At home, Adolf preaches abstinence. No girls. All they're after is to get themselves pregnant and get married. Learn a decent trade and establish yourself in the world. There's plenty of time for getting married. Jürgen doesn't understand what his father is making such a fuss about. He turns sixteen, and marriage is the last thing he has in mind.

Pels knows about Jürgen's girl friend. Have you laid her yet? Pels asks. Jürgen is evasive. Pels acts surprised. What do you mean? Is she playing hard to get?

Jürgen, too, is convinced that all girls are willing. It must be his fault. He pretends that he's been making it with her for a long time. Pels praises him: A true man of the world gets what he wants but doesn't brag about it.

Jürgen plays the man of the world.

Adolf is watching like a hawk now. The minute Jürgen begins to show the slightest interest in a girl, Adolf talks her down. That slut! I'd hate to guess how many guys she's slept with. Jürgen defends himself: I'm not after anything from her.

All I had to do was look at a girl, and he would tear her down, Jürgen says now.

·   ·   ·

Three months later, Jürgen still hasn't gotten anywhere with the girl. When she comes out of her house now, she says she has to run an errand for her mother.

In the first week in October, there is a traditional fishermen's festival in K., even though there haven't been any fish in the river for ages. People come from all over town and the surrounding country-side. There's a lot of heavy drinking, and the next morning drunks are sprawled out among the tents and stands. The boys comb the grounds early in the morning looking for lost coins. They also collect the used condoms strewn along the riverbanks, wash them out, and blow them up like balloons.

On Sunday morning there's an open-air concert in the square. A brass band plays marches. On the edge of the square a drunk is beating up a young man. Blood is running from the young man's mouth and nose. Every time he staggers to his feet, he is struck down again. Two men keep the spectators back. Let these two settle their own affairs. The drunk attacks again. Blood gushes from the young man's nose.

Jürgen is about to throw up. He staggers out of the crowd. Two burly concessionaires push their way through the spectators to break up the fight.

Jürgen doubles over to vomit. Someone takes hold of his shoulder. Through the tears in his eyes, he can see that it's the girl. A young man maybe two or three years older than Jürgen is standing a short distance away from her.

He sees the pair together later in the main tent.

A year later, Adolf tells him that the girl has to get married. Jürgen pretends he doesn't know whom he is talking about. Three or four years later, Jürgen runs into her in the park. She is eight or nine months pregnant. She's walking along with a small child on her one hand while she pushes a baby carriage with the other. She's lost her figure. She's twice as big as she used to be. Her legs are swollen and her breasts huge. Jürgen walks past her, pretending he doesn't know her.

.   .   .

Maybe, he says, if we had managed to get together back then, things might have gone differently for me and for her, too. But maybe I was just too young for her.

1 5   From the time Jürgen is twelve or thirteen, Adolf keeps demanding work of him. Jürgen isn't particularly interested. He would rather read or do puzzles and tinker by himself. His corner of the children's room is filled with model airplanes, tanks, and ships that he has built from kits. He likes to read utopian novels like *Land of Fire and Water* or historical tomes like *The Count of Monte Cristo* and *A Battle for Rome*. He doesn't know why he is so reluctant to do what Adolf asks. After he has been ordered over and over again, he grudgingly cleans out the cellar or attic, forks up the garden, or washes the car.

He never finishes any of his tasks, and Adolf is always dissatisfied. Whenever Jürgen simply refuses to do something or does it badly, Adolf bawls him out, calls him useless, and imposes penalties.

What Jürgen hates most is working with his father. He prefers to play with the tools. Adolf yells at him: Stop fooling around with those pliers and give me a hand here. Adolf is always asking him to hold on to something, and he criticizes Jürgen's awkwardness. If Jürgen stands too close, he snaps at him: Can't you stay out of my way?

And if Jürgen keeps his distance, his father also complains: Why are you just hanging around like that? Come here and watch how it's done.

If Jürgen accidentally bumps into the box of nails, Adolf scolds again: Watch where you're going, boy.

Adolf demands perfection.

He shows Jürgen how to do something. Jürgen watches listlessly. The expression on Jürgen's face is enough to drive Adolf wild. If I watched the way you do, I wouldn't learn anything either.

.   .   .

Sometimes Jürgen is allowed to do something himself, but Adolf's critical gaze over his shoulder makes him nervous. He bungles everything he attempts.

Adolf interrupts: Not that way! This way. Now, try again.

Jürgen does better this time, but he is too slow for Adolf, and his work isn't exacting enough. Okay, that's enough, son. Better let me do that. You're just not old enough for this yet. Hand me that piece of lath back there.

Adolf always needs an assistant. They are laying linoleum in the kitchen. Adolf is full of good advice: You can't be sloppy. You've got to pay attention to detail. Work well done is the best advertising a tradesman can have. You need the right tools for the right job. Skill isn't everything. The right attitude toward work and love of one's trade are important, too.

Jürgen hands him the lath. The experienced eye of the master slowly sights down the edge of it to check for straightness. Now the knife. I said the knife! Are you asleep on your feet?

Jürgen bends over to look for the knife. His eyes search the floor frantically; but, afraid that he won't find the knife quickly enough, he can hardly see anything at all. There's no knife to be found. Adolf groans. If I find it, you'll get a crack on the head. You kids don't even know how to use your eyes right.

Jürgen tries to make a little joke. Who do you mean by "you kids," Papa?

It's hard to say whether Adolf is annoyed about the joke or the knife. There doesn't seem to be any knife. Adolf reaches into his pocket and pulls out a longish object.

Oh, there it is. Now how was I to know that was a knife?

To cover up his own blunder, Adolf offers to explain to Jürgen how the knife works. The blade is inside the handle, and you use that button on the side to push it out.

Adolf tests the edge on the blade with his thumb. Jürgen wonders how he can check the blade for sharpness without cutting himself.

Now Adolf begins to cut the linoleum, using the lath as a straight-edge. After he's cut for a foot or so, the lath moves. The knife continues along the lath, making a bend in the cut.

Jürgen calls Adolf's attention to the mistake. Adolf snaps at him: I can see that for myself. Hold the other end of the lath down.

Adolf starts cutting again. This time the knife veers into the lath and ruins it.

Adolf wants to pick up the lath and turn it over. Jürgen, not understanding right away what Adolf wants to do, keeps bearing down on it. Adolf yanks it out of his hand so violently that he hurts him. Adolf's patience is at an end. It's Jürgen's own fault that he got hurt. Instead of paying attention, he stands around dreaming like an idiot.

In a rage, Adolf throws the lath aside and cuts freehand. Jürgen looks at the wavy line Adolf is cutting but doesn't say a word. Jürgen's critical look at a job that is obviously botched goads Adolf into a fury.

"What are you gawking at? Go get a piece of molding to cover up the edge!"

Later, at supper, Adolf praises his son. "Jürgen was a big help to me today."

"Is that right, Jürgen?" Edith asks. "All I heard was a lot of squabbling."

Jürgen bends over his plate and says nothing.

16 In the fall of 1965, Jürgen starts his apprenticeship.

His overall record in *Realschule* is satisfactory. He barely passes science with a *D*. In German, geography, history, social science, and religion he gets *B*'s. His only *A* is in music, his only failures in physical education and art. In speech and in English, his teachers give him the benefit of the doubt, and he gets *C*'s.

· · ·

Jürgen doesn't mention the *Gymnasium* anymore.

He turns sixteen, and his lower-middle-class family is an embarrassment to him. Pels's mother has never let him forget that he attends *Realschule* and not the *Gymnasium*. When Jürgen is with boys and girls in his class, he lies about his background and claims that his father is in the construction business. The others want to know whether his father is an architect or a building contractor. Jürgen lets them think his father has his own business and is a rich man.

When he is with people who know him, like Pels, he has to admit he goes to *Realschule*. On these occasions, he declares that a *Gymnasium* education would be of no use to him. He'll be taking over his father's business, and when the others are still studying, he'll already have a firm of his own.

He takes the Count of Monte Cristo as his model, a man of simple background who has been ennobled by persecution and great suffering. In some mysterious way, he has acquired great wealth. He is very pale and distinguished-looking, a lonely man, merciless toward those responsible for his misfortunes.

When Jürgen goes into a bar, he imagines himself surrounded by the aura of a tragic nobleman and thinks that he looks like the Count of Monte Cristo in the film. He forgets that he is wearing a faded plaid shirt, baggy pants with the cuffs above his ankles, and a stained and tattered corduroy jacket with sleeves that are too short for him. He has the feeling that the Count's large black cape is flowing from his shoulders.

He chooses a table away from the crowd and, in pretentious tones, orders a Coke. He makes conversation with the waiter and feels he successfully plays the hail-fellow. He hints that he comes from a well-to-do family. "So Daddy's in the chips, hmm?" the waiter remarks snidely. Jürgen fails to note the irony and feels flattered.

1 7 From the time he is fourteen, Jürgen takes piano lessons from Frau Pels.

She doesn't charge him for the first few lessons but offers them as a kind of charity to the underprivileged. She is the first in a long series of people who nourish the conviction in Jürgen that he does not have the right parents.

After the first few lessons, she offers, as a special favor, to teach him for only four marks an hour. Even a cleaning woman makes five marks or more. Jürgen gets an allowance of three marks per week. In 1959, when he was ten, he got his first allowance of one mark. Adolf has added half a mark each year.

Jürgen is willing to spend his entire allowance on the piano lessons, and all he asks of Adolf is the extra mark he doesn't have. Edith objects to giving it to him because Adolf makes her account for every last penny. That wouldn't be the end of it, she argues. We'll have to buy music and rent a piano, too.

Adolf agrees to pay for the piano lessons, but in exchange he reduces Jürgen's allowance to two marks per week. Edith complains bitterly: He throws money away on the children but makes me crawl for every penny.

Adolf also manages to get a piano for nothing. With the help of two of his workers and Uncle Erich, he horses the thing up two flights of stairs himself so that he won't have to pay a mover. Now the children's tiny room is crammed full.

Jürgen plays a lot but practices very little. He mainly uses the piano to express the unresolved conflicts in his personality. He sits at the keyboard for hours, sounds a note, plays a run, clumsily searches out a chord or a discord, and then sinks into a reverie.

If he is upset, he thrashes at the piano, pounds on the keys, produces nothing but cacophony. That's no way to play a piano, Adolf says.

Play something you've learned, Edith adds.

In Jürgen's mind, unrelated sounds express the misery of his life perfectly. The orderly runs and chords of his études and sonatinas mean nothing to him; he can't express himself through them.

After a few months, he starts composing music. He buys large sheets of music paper with sixteen staffs on them and, after picking out tunes on the piano, writes down parts for different instruments.

All night long he broods over his score. Night is over at six in the morning when the Schütrumpfs get up. The only aids to composition he has are an old treatise on harmony that he has borrowed and a guide to instruments. From this guide he determines what clef he should use for each instrument. When he plays a passage he has written, he bursts into tears.

He entitles his first composition "Dirge on the Death of the World Spirit." In the week before Easter, he sends the prelude to this work to the local radio station and asks that it be played on Good Friday. He spends Good Friday glued to the radio. His parents don't know what to make of him. The World Spirit is Jürgen himself.

1 8   Wagner and Beethoven are his heroes. He goes to the city library and takes out a book with excerpts from Wagnerian scores in it. In his own compositions, he uses all the instruments of a Wagnerian orchestra. He makes a point of mentioning that the piece he sent to the radio station called for a hundred and thirty-two musicians.

Beethoven appeals to him more as a personality. A film starring Ewald Balser as Beethoven is shown in the auditorium of Jürgen's trade school. He has forgotten the title. His schoolmates are bored to death, but he is enthralled.

Beethoven is shown walking through a lonely landscape. His hair is tousled, and he makes wild gestures as if he were composing music in his mind. A storm is raging. Thunder rolls; lightning strikes. An orchestra is playing passages from the *Pastoral Symphony*. The viewer gets the impression that the music is coming straight out of the composer's head and is a direct product of his gestures and his tumultuous spirit.

In the fall, Jürgen gets a new coat. He insists on a generously cut loden coat because it reminds him of the coat Beethoven wore. That weekend, he rides the trolley to the end of the line and walks out into the fields. He uses a pencil as a baton and gesticulates wildly with it, pretending that he is Beethoven in the film.

If anybody had seen me, he remarks now, they would have thought I was crazy.

Jürgen owes his love of music and whatever musical knowledge he has to Pels. Frau Pels comes from a good family. Unlike Jürgen's mother, she is the head of her household. Herr Pels is small and always seems intimidated, especially when his wife speaks. Jürgen can't remember ever hearing Herr Pels say anything.

Frau Pels encourages Pels's interest in music.

One day, Pels plays a short piece for Jürgen. Jürgen suspects that Pels has written it himself, and he asks uneasily who the composer is. Pels indicates that he wrote the piece. Jürgen follows his lead and becomes so caught up in his image of himself as a brilliant composer that it takes on pathological qualities.

It is Pels's idea to hear all the Wagner operas that are broadcast on the radio. The broadcasts from distant stations often come in very badly and are marred by constant static. The boys huddle around the radio and sit by it for hours, no matter how poor the quality of the broadcast.

Jürgen goes overboard in his enthusiasm for Wagner. When Pels's family moves to Bamberg, Pels says he'll be able to go to Bayreuth now. Jürgen asks him to send an ivy leaf from the master's grave. He wants a huge beret for his birthday.

"Now what do you suppose that's all about?" Edith says. "He's had that silly thing on all day."

. . .

He takes out all the books the library has on Wagner. Wagner's life strikes him as exemplary. He spent money hand over fist on traveling and high living and never worried where he'd get more, Jürgen says. He did what he pleased.

Jürgen admires Wagner's refusal to conform, his unconventional artist's life, the way he made off with his friend's wife and let other people support him as if it must have been an honor for them to pay for his silk underwear, the way he convinced even a king to finance his schemes.

Jürgen does not have much understanding of Wagner's music. He is enthusiastic about the leitmotivs.

> Whoever fears the point of my spear
> Will never pass through these flames.

Jürgen can still quote lines like that and sing the music that goes with them.

He is also impressed by thunderous orchestral attacks, by musical storms. At those passages he would turn the radio all the way up: the overture to *Lohengrin*, the singers' processional to the Wartburg, the prelude to the third act of *Die Meistersinger*.

1 9   Jürgen's attempts to resist his apprenticeship as a plumber are as outrageous as they are unsuccessful. Although he shows no great talent for the piano, he claims that the manual work he has to do is interfering with his progress as a pianist. He says that it's essential for a composer and conductor to be a first-rate pianist as well.

Having to get up so early and work so hard physically takes such a toll on his intellectual reserves, he says, that he has no energy left for composing. He feels he is destined to be an artist and sees himself as an exceptionally talented man with a great future before him.

He cites his left-handedness as proof of his artistic leanings. He is actually right-handed, but he has heard that geniuses are often left-handed. Adolf is disgusted. The fact is that Jürgen is not very adept with his left hand, and his attempt to use it only makes him more awkward than ever.

He claims that he faints often and is prone to vertigo. He considers his labile temperament a sign of budding genius, and he manages to convince himself that he loses consciousness easily.

He is daydreaming as usual at a piano concert in Murhardt Hall. The music serves as a background for his fantasies. When the third movement of a sonata ends, he thinks the piece is over and begins to clap. The people sitting nearby stare icily at him. The blood rushes to his head; everything starts to whirl before his eyes; his ears ring; he feels dizzy. Then he passes out. He wakes up on a bench in the lobby. An elderly woman who works in the cloakroom is patting his cheek and saying, "There, there, you'll be just fine now."

Adolf doesn't take Jürgen's complaints seriously.

He says he used to know a cabinetmaker who worked like a horse but still managed to be an excellent organist. Jürgen himself knows a man called Eigenbrodt, who is a good violinist. When the sports club Tuspo 96 has its Christmas party in the back room of the Gasthaus zur Mitte, Eigenbrodt plays with piano and drum accompaniment. He plays at other club and family gatherings, too.

One day when some workers are laying a new sidewalk along Frankfurter Strasse, Jürgen spots Eigenbrodt among them. Eigenbrodt is carrying a heavy curbstone. It occurs to Jürgen that a lack of talent may account for his own slow progress with the piano. That only increases his aversion for his parents. He thinks musical ability and genius are inherited traits.

2 0   About a month after Jürgen begins his apprenticeship, his mother tells him she has spoken with the music teacher in a *Gymnasium*. He has agreed to hear Jürgen play and to look at his composi-

tions. Jürgen is a bit hesitant. He thinks it's too soon for that. Adolf is willing to send Jürgen to the *Gymnasium* and to let him take lessons at the conservatory as well if the music teacher recommends it.

For a week, Jürgen practices piano for hours every evening after work, and he works feverishly into the night on a score so that he will have a finished composition to offer. In most of the score, the orchestra plays long, drawn-out notes while three harps play arpeggios.

The music teacher has not a good word for Jürgen's composition. A musician in an orchestra may be willing to play one note for minutes at a time every once in a while if the other instruments are doing something interesting. But Jürgen's composition is completely lacking in musical ideas and is nothing but a pointless heaping together of innumerable notes.

In view of Jürgen's age, it is unlikely that his talent for the piano will develop significantly. The teacher suggests that Jürgen become a music teacher if he has his heart set on a career in music. He doesn't have the talent to become a performing musician.

This hits Jürgen like a death sentence, and his adolescent rage and despair rise to a fever pitch. His diary is filled with ominous threats and accusations directed against himself, his parents, humanity, his time, the whole world. The main afflictions that are destroying him, he feels, are his compulsion to masturbate constantly; the people who fail to recognize his genius; the age he lives in, an age in which genius can no longer flourish; a world doomed to destruction; the vanity, superficiality, and materialism of mankind.

He writes over and over again that he will punish the world by committing suicide. He plans to arrange his suicide so that it will look like murder. He also considers writing a farewell letter that will lay the blame for his death on his parents. At other times, he thinks about disappearing without leaving a clue to his whereabouts.

One evening, his mother asks if he doesn't sometimes wish he lived in another age, could be a different person, and had different parents. Jürgen's answer is evasive. He goes into the children's room and pulls out his diary from behind his old schoolbooks. He has made a habit of sticking the filled pages together with Scotch tape. On the cover he has written a note saying the diary may not be opened until after his death.

The tape has been cut. He acts as though nothing has happened. At first he is outraged by this violation of his privacy. Then his shame and outrage give way to spiteful pleasure. He is glad that his parents know what he thinks of them and that he has a pathological need to masturbate. His plans for suicide must worry them a lot.

He imagines how they lie in bed at night and talk for hours, trying to figure out where they went wrong; one night Edith confesses that Jürgen is not Adolf's child after all. His real father is a baron and the owner of a manor in northern Hesse. Adolf's first reaction is rage, but then he comes around to reason. Jürgen's parents finally decide to send the boy to live with his natural father, who will surely want to have him. At last, Jürgen will be able to live a life in keeping with his talents and inclinations.

2 1   Jürgen still remembers his apprenticeship in his father's business as a nightmare.

Adolf was strict enough when he tried to press Jürgen and Herbert into service at home. He once hit Jürgen in the back with a big clump of dirt when Jürgen refused to dig up the garden.

He often tried to get the boys to work by scolding them.

"I'm not your servant!" he would yell. "Do you think your mother and I feel like waiting on you hand and foot? If you want to be warm, you can lug some coal up from the cellar, too."

But on the whole he let them play and do what they liked. When he felt overworked, he would make them help him, even though their help was of little use to him. At these times he would throw all their things together into a pile in their room and make them put the things away again. And do it right this time, he would bellow, not the way it was before.

But, Jürgen recalls, he could also be affectionate. He would take them in his arms and squeeze them against his big belly. Jürgen's most vivid memories of his father are the sense of safety he felt in his father's embrace, his father's smell, and his soft, friendly voice.

As a teacher, Adolf is a tyrant intent on humiliating Jürgen. He is particularly strict and unjust when customers or other workers are present. He throws things at Jürgen if he doesn't move quickly enough. In his first few months as an apprentice, Jürgen isn't allowed to do anything but dirty work from which he learns nothing.

At home, Adolf rarely swears, but with his apprentices he often uses foul and insulting language.

"I ought to crack your nuts for you. You sad sack, you tub of shit. Come here, you numbskull. I'll work you till the shit runs down your leg. I'll shape you up if I have to kick your ass from hell to breakfast."

He tells other people you can't handle boys with kid gloves if you want to make anything out of them. This kind of talk annoys Jürgen because he feels it doesn't reflect Adolf's true nature. He thinks his father is just showing off.

Adolf is easier on the other apprentice who started working at the same time Jürgen did. The boys in trade school call this other apprentice "Käse." Käse is a head taller than Jürgen and works like a horse. Why can't you be like Käse there? Adolf says. He can rip a pipe out of a wall in the time it takes you to get your tools together.

Jürgen is superior to Käse only on Saturdays. On Saturdays it's Jürgen who sets a good example. Käse's father works for the city in the sewer system. With the sewer rats, Adolf calls it.

·　　·　　·

In the first year of their apprenticeship, the two boys get an hour's instruction every Saturday on how to deal with customers. Adolf explains in great detail how to approach a customer's door.

"You put down your ladder and toolbox, dust your shoes off with a rag, take your handkerchief out of your pocket and blow your nose, check whether your fly is zipped up, and comb your hair."

"If you don't have a comb, your fingers will do. . . . You carry your cap in your hand. . . . Do you have a handkerchief? Let's see it. . . . You call this old snot rag a handkerchief? . . . Now for the comb. . . . That's no comb. All that rusty thing is fit for is raking out lice. Okay, let's go over it again. What do you do before you ring a customer's doorbell?"

Käse stutters. Adolf makes him write it all down and memorize it. After the second hour, Jürgen can recite the whole routine by heart. It takes weeks before Käse has learned it all without forgetting something. Adolf checks his hands for cleanliness before they all sit down to eat. He also inspects Käse's lunch before he lets him go out on a job with another worker: I don't let anybody on my crews take stinking cheese sandwiches into a customer's house. This is meant for the ears of his regular employees, too, but he doesn't dare to inspect their lunchboxes.

Finally the two apprentices are allowed to ring a customer's doorbell for the first time. Adolf stands out of sight on the landing below and checks out their performance.

There were a lot of things he didn't realize about his father until he started his apprenticeship, Jürgen says now. That's when he first really got to know his father.

Adolf was an opportunist who made up to people in a way that offended Jürgen. At home and with his friends, Adolf always played the big boss; but when he was with customers, he suddenly became a pathetic figure who was hopelessly insecure and whose big talk was nothing but show.

A few years later, Jürgen comes to love his father for these very reasons.

2 2 In the late summer of 1967, when Jürgen turns eighteen and has almost completed the second year of his apprenticeship, he develops an interest in philosophy.

Once again he takes his inspiration from Pels. Pels has just graduated from the *Gymnasium* and is spending a week of his summer in N.

Jürgen meets him at the train station. Pels is in high spirits and soon has everyone on the platform staring at him. In the concourse, he announces that he is inviting all his old friends to the Gasthaus zur Mitte that evening. He pulls a bundle of five- and ten-mark notes out of his pocket, throws them up in the air, and lets them flutter down to the floor.

Then he crawls around on all fours, barking like a dog and picking up the money.

He earned the money working on a construction job during vacation. Jürgen is embarrassed by Pels's performance.

The very prospect of Pels's visit has caused trouble at the Schütrumpfs'. Edith refuses to take Pels in as a guest. She just can't do it on the household money she's getting. If Pels is going to stay with them, Adolf has to give her more. Adolf doesn't see why he should feed that "Jew boy."

Jürgen sulks. They begrudge him the one real friendship he has, he says, and Pels's parents aren't Jews at all.

Adolf mutters that he doesn't give a damn. Finally, Jürgen offers to pay for Pels's stay. Jürgen's pay as an apprentice is twenty marks per week. Most of this money goes to Edith for room and board. The rest he saves for new clothes and incidentals. He has to give up his money for two weeks to cover the cost of Pels's one-week visit.

Jürgen still gets angry when he thinks back on how his parents cheated him. And then to make matters worse, Edith pinched pennies more than ever on food that week. For breakfast there was nothing but margarine and plum jam on bread. At noon, it was some nondescript stew or casserole. At supper, she counted out slices of wurst and cheese.

One of the things Pels takes out of his rucksack when he unpacks is a biography of Wagner. It was written by an Englishman called Chamberlain, who was married to one of Wagner's daughters. Jürgen finds this book overpowering. He had never realized before how philosophically profound Wagner was.

That evening Jürgen and Pels go to the Gasthaus zur Mitte, and Pels treats all his old friends. He gets drunk and lets the others do what they will with him. They set him on a chair and soap up his face with a beer brush. Later, Jürgen tells his friend he thought the whole thing was degrading.

After a few days, Pels runs out of money. He makes a deal with Lothar, the innkeeper's son. If Pels drinks a beer glass full of spit, Lothar's father will give Pels and his friends anything they want on the house. Everybody takes a turn spitting into the beer glass. The faces of the boys express a mixture of excitement, sadism, and disgust. When Pels raises the glass to his lips, some of them turn away. Others watch with a pained expression and press their hands to their stomachs.

Jürgen is hypnotized by the spectacle. He has the feeling that he himself is drinking out of the glass. His throat closes; his stomach turns. As Pels drains the last slimy strands from the glass, Jürgen's legs go wobbly under him. He stumbles out of the room. In the alleyway outside he throws up. He vomits with such force that he feels his cheeks won't stand the pressure. His stomach and throat are racked with cramps. Tears rush to his eyes. The pounding of the blood in his head is intolerable. His eyes remain bloodshot for days.

After a while he goes back into the bar. The mere sight of the room, the glasses, his friends drinking makes him feel sick again. Pels is the hero of the evening, but behind his back the others feel nothing but disgust toward him. How can anybody sink so low, they say. Jürgen hands him a key. He doesn't feel well. He's going home.

Pels leaves the next day. Just the sight of his friend is enough to give Jürgen the shivers. They make a date to go to the Bayreuth festival next year. Jürgen gets Chamberlain's Wagner biography from the state library in K. One by one he reads all the authors that were supposed to have influenced Wagner.

Nietzsche makes a particularly strong impression on him. He doesn't understand what Nietzsche is saying and thinks his ideas are all crazy. What impresses him is the sense of a world view that rises above earthly concerns and of a personal perspective that elevates this philosopher above all men.

Nietzsche would have understood Jürgen. They are kindred souls, both at a great remove from all mankind. When Jürgen picks up his heavy toolbox in the morning and sets out for work, tired, sick, pale, shivering, his stomach aching and his eyes tearing, he asks himself what great things fate may have in store for him. Someday he himself may be the World Spirit that understands everything in the world and knows what keeps it in motion, the spirit that judges, condemns, and redeems, dispensing punishment and granting mercy.

Someday a mere thought of his will suffice to kill people and annihilate whole empires.

He takes pills for his headaches. After his death, people will say that toward the end he could only keep himself going with pills. It's hard to believe that he could work at all and lead an outwardly normal life.

2 3   Toward the end of his apprenticeship—Jürgen has just turned nineteen—the turmoil of his adolescent years begins to subside.

He says he realized only years later how crazy he had been then. He had undergone many changes, but he can't really account for any of them. Everything could have gone one way just as easily as another.

In the spring of 1968, he gets to know a girl. He has enrolled in a French course in an adult-education program. Twice a week he takes a trolley to K. at seven in the evening. All the other students are women. Some of them are quite a bit older than he. Most of them seem to be married.

Jürgen sits down alone in the back of the room. The teacher asks him to move up to the front. Faced with the choice of sitting next to an older, motherly-looking woman or a mousy girl, he sits down next to the girl. Half an hour later, a middle-aged man joins the class. As it turns out, he is a driving instructor. His name is Pogunke.

Jürgen claims that the girl struck him as being incredibly ugly. At times when she thought no one was looking at her, she had an almost idiotic expression on her face. Her blonde hair was done up in a permanent wave. Her dresses, blouses, and skirts looked like hand-me-downs from her mother. She didn't wear makeup, but her skin was very pale and delicate.

During the first class, he accidentally touches her with his elbow. The place he touches feels soft. He notices how she jumps and pulls away from him. He is startled, too, and pulls his arm back as if he had been burned. He tries not to look at her. When he does glance at her several minutes later, she is looking straight ahead.

At the second class, he decides to speak to her. For the first half hour he wonders what he can say. He can hardly follow what the teacher is saying. When someone turns the doorknob, he says involuntarily and more to himself than to anyone else: I bet that's Herr Pogunke.

It is Herr Pogunke. The girl smiles. Jürgen thinks she can look pretty sometimes. He keeps sneaking glances at her. After a while he dares to look at her breasts. She seems to have small breasts. After class he

helps her into her coat. He asks her in an offhand way if he can walk
with her for a bit.

She lives in Kuhberg on the hillside above N. He says that's not out of
his way. They ride to the end of the line on the trolley. It's still a
fifteen-minute walk to her house. They pass through a small woods
on the way. They talk about the course, the people in it, and the
teacher. They find themselves agreeing on most things. Jürgen notices
with surprise that he has no desire to disagree with her. If he tries to
put on one of his airs, she won't stand for it.

He is ready to change all his ways.

She works as a secretary in a bank. She wanted to go to the
Gymnasium, but her father was against it. She would just get mar-
ried anyhow. She had to save so much every month for her dowry.
That's why she only went to *Realschule,* too.

When they get to her house, Jürgen is surprised. The house is almost
a villa and has a large yard. Is this where you live? Jürgen says. I
don't even know your name yet.

Her name is Ilse Gutberlet.

When he gets home, he writes her a letter, but he doesn't dare to send
it. He writes more letters to her on the following evenings. After their
next class, he gives her the letters. She has written to him, too. They
read each other's letters on the trolley.

Jürgen describes his background and his parents in amusing terms.
He presents his parents as simple but good-natured people who enjoy
life and who are all the more lovable for their little weaknesses. He
owes them a great deal. He incorporates this information into a
description of an evening at home.

Ilse takes his hand. It doesn't matter to her what his background is.
As they walk to her house, she tells about her family. Her father is a
business consultant.

He earns a lot but doesn't show off with his wealth.

He puts his money into things of lasting value, like expensive furniture and rugs. While everybody else was dealing in food and liquor and tobacco in the black-market days, he was accumulating silverware and jewelry. He made the most of his opportunities. When the time comes, he wants her to marry a student who belongs to a good fraternity.

Ilse and her mother have their clothes custom made by a seamstress. Her father and brother go to a tailor. One shouldn't be able to tell how much a piece of clothing cost by looking at it. Quality and workmanship are what matter. Her brother is already a lot like her father. Last Sunday they walked up and down in the yard together with their hats on but in their shirt-sleeves. Her brother is taking a commercial course now. He has to finish that before he'll be allowed to go to the university.

When Gutberlet asked her mother to marry him, her mother asked him to give her a day to think about it. Her father was very offended by this.

Ilse isn't allowed to go out alone. The French course is an exception. If Father knew that she lets Jürgen walk her home! When Father's cigarette goes out, he says: This is one of those housemaid cigarettes. It goes out by itself, just like a housemaid.

They had always had a maid until just a few years ago. That was money down the drain. The maids never did any work, and they stole everything they could get their hands on.

But you can go out with a girl friend, Jürgen says. No, she can't do that either. Besides, she doesn't have a girl friend. Most girls are no good and have boyfriends by the time they're sixteen.

Jürgen is impressed. When he gets home, he writes her that he is planning to go to engineering school when he has finished his apprenticeship. He has always hoped he would meet someone like her and he asks if he may kiss her.

In the trolley, she gives him a letter she wrote during class. He may.

.   .   .

Afterwards, in the woods, when they kiss and press their bodies together, Jürgen runs his hand up under her suit jacket and feels one of her breasts. It's smaller than he thought.

2 4   Jürgen changes for Ilse's sake. He decides to become an engineer. He is preoccupied with fantasies about Ilse's family. In one of his daydreams, Gutberlet throws him out of the house. His daughter is too good for a plumber. In another one, Jürgen pulls up in front of the house in his car. He hands the maid his card: Jürgen Schütrumpf, Engineer.

The maid takes him into the living room. Jürgen has a well-paying job. Ilse's father offers him a cigar and gets out a bottle of cognac. They sit back in big leather armchairs. The décor of the room is English in style. Ilse's mother is sitting on the edge of her chair at the dining-room table. You'll join us for dinner, Herr Schütrumpf, won't you? Gutberlet asks. If it's not too much trouble, Jürgen replies. Gutberlet sends his wife into the kitchen with a wave of his hand.

Later, Ilse's father suggests that she show Jürgen the garden. An Airedale accompanies them.
    At dinner, Jürgen meets Ilse's brother Rainer. He has a haughty manner and immaculate long white hands like those of a pianist. He watches condescendingly as Jürgen struggles to serve himself without spilling any food on the tablecloth.

After the meal, Jürgen hides his hands under the table. His fingernails are broken, and the grime is so deeply embedded in the skin of his fingers that even hand cleanser won't get it out. His hands are covered with nicks and cuts.

Where did you study? Rainer asks. Here in K., Jürgen replies. I didn't realize that we had an institute of technology here, Rainer says. It's an engineering school, Jürgen says. Aha, says Rainer, then you're not a real engineer at all. Frau Gutberlet says: Rainer!

"Care for a cigarette?" Rainer asks, holding out a silver cigarette case to Jürgen.

One day they come upon a couple making love. The path through the woods is unlit. Something moves ahead of them on the side of the path. Not suspecting anything, they keep on walking toward it.

The man is on top of the woman. He raises himself up on his arms and looks in the direction of the footsteps. When he catches sight of Jürgen and Ilse, he falls forward and hides his face on the woman's shoulder. The woman covers her face with her hands. Her white legs rise up on either side of the man's body. They seem extraordinarily long and naked to Jürgen, but the couple's bodies are almost invisible against the dark, moist ground of the woods.

Jürgen has only one thought. Ilse. This scene will be so offensive to her that she'll never want to sleep with him. Ilse seizes his arm, leans her head against his chest, and goes past the couple turned away from them. She doesn't say anything. All she does is utter a little cry of disgust. She never talks about the incident later. According to Jürgen, it was a crucial experience for her. The whole tone of their sexual relationship was established that evening.

2 5   The woods is also the scene of Jürgen and Ilse's first sexual experiments. They sit in a close embrace on a bench and kiss each other hungrily. Jürgen's left hand is on her right breast. He reaches across in front of her with his right hand and, trying to make it seem unintentional, guides hers to his penis.

He does this several times because she keeps pulling her hand back. After a while, he unzips his fly, puts her hand on his penis, holds her hand firmly in place there, and moves it up and down. She seems willing to do this for a few seconds. Then she stands up quickly. She has to go home, she says.

.   .   .

Jürgen refuses to go with her. If she insists on walking through the dark woods alone, she can. He's going to stay. She goes off by herself. A little later he gets up and runs after her. Sobbing, she throws herself into his arms. He mustn't leave her. She has no one but him.

After their next French class, he puts her hand on his penis again. This time she gives in. He is proud. If Pels only knew. He lets go of Ilse and leans back, the way Pels used to when Jürgen masturbated him. Ilse asks him to hold her and kiss her. Jürgen never did that when he brought Pels to orgasm. He reaches up under her skirt and strokes her. She moans softly. Jürgen feels her getting wet.

When he gets home, he is filled with a great sense of satisfaction. With Pels, the satisfaction was always one-sided. Jürgen feels that he doesn't need much to be happy. But a woman is one thing he needs.

In the following weeks, Jürgen keeps trying to convince Ilse to sleep with him. She refuses. She's still a virgin, she insists. Once, she takes his hand and lets him feel her hymen with his finger. He claims he can't feel it. When he threatens to break the hymen with his finger, she stands up and slaps him.

She was awfully prudish, he says. She didn't want to sleep with a man until her wedding night. That's the way she was brought up. Her father never would have married a woman who had had a sexual relationship before marriage.

A few weeks later, Gutberlet takes Ilse to a gynecologist for an examination.

At Easter time, Adolf and Edith go on a vacation to Austria, visiting an old army friend of Adolf's. Jürgen invites Ilse to his house. They cut their French class. He buys a bottle of cheap red wine and makes mulled wine.

Later in the evening, he asks Ilse to take off her clothes and get in bed. He threatens never to see her again. She takes off her sweater. She keeps her slip and bra on. She pulls up her skirt but keeps her panties on. Jürgen takes out his penis, lies on top of her, kisses her, and tries to slip his penis past her underwear and into her vagina. The moment he thinks he's inside, it's all over. He ejaculates.

In the weeks that follow, they do this after almost every class. They do it lying down between the desks in a dark empty classroom before the school is locked up. They do it standing against a tree in the park. They do it on an old couch in the toolshed in her parents' yard. She lifts her skirt and squeezes his penis between her thighs. She never takes off her underwear. He never penetrates her.

After a few weeks they have a fight over this. He threatens to rip her panties off. She says that if he ever tries to take her by force, she'll report him to the police. He once threatens to sleep with someone else. She answers that if he is unfaithful to her, she'll leave him. But before she does, she'll sleep with him so that he'll know what he's losing.

Jürgen has his first sexual intercourse with a prostitute in the late summer of 1968. He takes thirty marks out of his bank account. For days on end, he haunts the street in K. where prostitutes wait for customers in cars to pick them up. The minute a woman talks to him, he looks right through her and walks away. A fat woman of about fifty seems approachable to him. She has immense breasts and wants fifty marks.

Jürgen gives her thirty. She leads him through a stale-smelling corridor into the courtyard of an old building. The wings of the building and the house in the yard seem to be unoccupied. There is a low shed with a metal roof in one corner of the courtyard. Inside, there is a mattress. She pulls out a condom, stuffs her panties in her handbag, lies down, and spreads her legs.

Jürgen stands there paralyzed. Her efficient, businesslike manner leaves him stunned. He'd like to take the initiative himself. At the same time, he's all worked up over the prospect of penetrating a woman for the first time. His penis is throbbing as if he had an infection in it. He feels that he is going to ejaculate any minute. The woman signals to him impatiently. Come on. Do you think I want to lie here forever for your lousy thirty marks?

When Jürgen leans over her, she spits on her hands and rubs them together. Then she takes his penis and guides him into her. The inside of her vagina seems immense. She thrusts rapidly with her hips to make him come. When he tries to kiss her, she turns her head to one side. After a few thrusts, he ejaculates.

See? she says. It wasn't so bad after all, was it? If you feel like it again sometime, come see me. I'll give you a special price. She leaves while Jürgen is zipping up his pants. He looks around on the floor as if he were afraid he had forgotten something. But he can't see anything in the dark.

He goes to the Gasthaus zur Mitte that evening feeling like a new man. Believe it or not, he says, I felt really proud of myself, even though the business with that old slut was horrible. He looks ready to take on the world and stands old Penzing, the innkeeper, to a drink. When Penzing asks him where he's been, he answers: Where do you think? He squeezes his thumb between his middle and index fingers and says: A man's got to have it now and then.

At trade school, he tells the others how he made it recently with a huge woman. He describes her mammoth breasts. He doesn't mention that she was a prostitute, but he does say that she was older. The boys think sleeping with an older woman is a special triumph, particularly if she's married.

2 6   Jürgen and Pels see each other for the last time this summer. It's vacation time, even for the trade school, and Adolf gives his son a few days off.

They have agreed to meet in Bayreuth. Jürgen hitchhikes. He has sent his suit ahead to general delivery. He gets as far as Würzburg the first day. On the second, he reaches Bayreuth. At the entrance of the youth hostel, he runs into Pels, who has been there since noon. They take a shower together, talk nonsense, and laugh themselves into a fit.

They have a day to pass before they see their first performance. Jürgen had his tickets sent to him by mail. Late in the afternoon they go to the theater. The street is lined with curious onlookers. The people going to the theater have to pass through this lane. A steady procession of expensive cars creeps up the hill.

Pels finds the scene fascinating. Jürgen is disgusted by it. The people on the hill strike him as guests at a party closed to the public. He feels the Bayreuth theater is a temple that should be approached with humility and modesty. Pels disagrees. Wagner's music was written for the élite, not for the masses, who are stupid, insensitive, and unable to appreciate beauty. Later on, Pels starts talking politics. He has joined the CDU.* Jürgen can't understand him. Politics is a dirty business, he says.

Their argument is so bitter that they almost go their separate ways. Pels defends the crowd up on the hill. Jürgen accuses him of coming to Bayreuth just so he can feel he's part of that crowd for two evenings.

The performances are a disappointment to Jürgen, too. He has a poor seat. He is right behind a pillar and can't see the stage. Whenever he leans to one side to look around it, the people behind him complain. He doesn't like the staging. He prefers the realistic sets they have in the theater in K.

Even the music strikes him as new and unfamiliar. The emotional impact is missing. You could hear all the instruments individually, he says.

*Christlich-Demokratische Union—TRANS.

. . .

A few weeks later, Jürgen receives a short, handwritten note. Pels is dead. He had a heart defect and simply fell over dead. No one had been aware of this condition at all. Jürgen writes to Frau Pels and tells her what her son meant to him. He cries as he writes. The next day he tears the letter up.

He had exaggerated in the letter. He hadn't felt any great love for Pels, who was not really such a remarkable person after all. He admits that Pels introduced him to many things. But the fact of the matter is that Pels was a shrewd con artist who had a *Gymnasium* education and looked like a violin player in a Vienna coffeehouse. He was no good, and all he did for Jürgen was give him big ideas.

2 7   By late fall, Ilse too has passed out of Jürgen's life.

While they are waiting at a trolley stop, Jürgen issues an ultimatum: either she sleeps with him right or it's all over. She refuses again, but she gives him a long, lingering kiss. He tears himself away from her and runs off. A few blocks down the street, he goes into a telephone booth and starts masturbating.

Suddenly the door flies open. It's Ilse. He's so ashamed that he doesn't know what to say and just runs away. Two weeks later, he gets a letter. She is inviting him for coffee on Sunday afternoon.

The invitation inspires a wave of exaggerated self-esteem in him. This invitation marks the beginning of his steady rise into better social circles. In his long daydreams, he sees a brilliant future opening up before him: social status, people who call on him to ask favors, a responsible position, money, a big car, a big house, Ilse wearing an expensive gown as she receives their guests while he stays in the background and appears only when everyone is there. He enters the room like a star coming on stage.

. . .

His daydreams end harshly when reality intrudes on him again: his father's workshop, the plumber's snake he is using to ream bucketfuls of shit out of a clogged drainpipe, the oilcloth on the kitchen table, the plates with food slopped onto them, his parents' underwear drying over the bathtub, a glance into the mirror.

He is often on the verge of declining the invitation. He doesn't like himself. His voice is grating. His hair is greasy. He has several big pimples on his face and neck. His suits don't fit him and are ugly. He has only one pair of oxfords, and they have heavy crêpe rubber soles. They're not elegant shoes.

He doesn't know how he should behave. He has adopted a few poses that he has seen on television, gotten from books, or copied from other people. He doesn't know what he is like himself.

I never knew whether I existed at all, he says.

The way he acts at home with his parents and Herbert or at work with Käse and the other men never seems to be an expression of his true self.

He decides to play the silent bohemian type who sees through the pretenses of the world, looks down on it, and is weary of it. This way he won't have to worry about his clothes.

He goes without shaving for several days. On Sunday he doesn't even comb his hair. He puts on his work clothes. What? You're going looking like that? Edith asks in horror. Leave me alone. I've got to go.

The afternoon is a huge disappointment. The Gutberlets turn out to be petty philistines with no feeling for higher values. Gutberlet puts on airs. He talks with his wife about his business successes as though Jürgen weren't even there. The way he talks, you'd think he saved his family from financial ruin every day.

Frau Gutberlet is fussy and irritable. She makes derogatory remarks about her husband. Gutberlet strikes back in an almost insulting way. They are on the verge of a family squabble. Ilse shows Jürgen how much her father loves her. She kept buttering him up and calling him Daddy, Jürgen says. It all seemed false and artificial. He preferred the honest rage of his own parents' fights.

Jürgen plays the nihilist. He rejects money, cars, the institution of the family. He'll probably never marry. He doesn't want to achieve anything in life. Anyone who gets somewhere in politics or business these days is a crook. The only true values are intellectual and artistic. His models are the *clochards* of Paris, the medieval hermits, Diogenes in his tub.

Tchaikovsky, who drank a glass of contaminated water from the Moskva after capturing the mood of his waning years in music. Beethoven, who went deaf so that he would no longer have to hear the clamor of the world but only his own music. That kind of deafness was ordained by the gods.

You have a lot to learn, young man, Gutberlet says. If everybody thought the way you do, the world would soon grind to a halt. The vanity and rapaciousness of men are destroying the world, Jürgen answers. He lays his hands flat on the table, closes his eyes, begins to stutter, and pretends that he is a medium. He is copying a man named Udo, who sometimes comes to the Gasthaus zur Mitte and fascinates the crowd there with his performances.

He has a vision of humanity annihilating itself with greed. He sees a world devoid of human life. Only after the extinction of the human race will peace return to earth.

"Go put on your show somewhere else," says Gutberlet.

"I think what he's saying is very interesting," Frau Gutberlet says.

Gutberlet gets up and leaves.

Ilse's brother talks about nothing but his car. He is wearing immaculate light yellow pants and a dark blazer. He has a gold cigarette lighter.

"After I finish at the university," he says, "I'll go into business." Jürgen says that he is a philosopher. Or he may decide to become a composer. He was in Bayreuth this summer.

Ilse's brother says that he took a guided tour through North Africa on his vacation.

Later, Frau Gutberlet sets a place for Jürgen and serves him scrambled eggs with home fries. You can't go home without having something to eat, she says. Jürgen eats, nearly choking with embarrassment, as the three Gutberlets watch him.

When he gets home, he writes Ilse that he is breaking off with her. He has no use for a girl who comes from such a mediocre background and is unable to free herself from her family. That is an allusion to her refusal to sleep with him.

He has a rough road ahead of him, but it will take him to the very top.

2 8   On October 1, 1968, Jürgen takes the test for his journeyman's license in plumbing and heating. So does Käse. Jürgen gets "satisfactory" on the practical part of his exam, "good" on the theoretical part. Käse's grades are just the other way around: theoretical "satisfactory"; practical "good." They get along well together at work.

Käse and his father and brother-in-law are building a house in their spare time. Just in case, he says. Sometimes you get married sooner than you think.

Jürgen visits him now and then in his village a few kilometers outside of K. Käse is a big shot out there. He's president of the young men's committee that organizes the village fairs, he sings first tenor in the men's glee club. He's a squad leader in the volunteer fire department. He also belongs to the Nimrod Rifle Club and the bowling club, and he plays on the local soccer team. He had a big belly, drank like a fish, and had built himself a car out of junk parts by the time he was nineteen, Jürgen says. Guys in the villages do that kind of thing.

Sometimes he envies Käse. Käse didn't have any problems. If he didn't like something, he'd curse and complain about it. Sometimes he got into fights. Every Saturday he went to a fair or dance somewhere. He had reclining seats in his car and was always after girls.

Once they have taken their journeymen's licenses, Käse regards Jürgen as the junior boss. When Jürgen and Käse began the third year of their apprenticeships, Adolf let one of his two workers go. Now he dismisses the other one and takes on only one new apprentice.

Adolf's attitude toward Jürgen changes practically overnight after Jürgen takes his journeyman's license. Jürgen has proved himself. Adolf pays him as much as he pays Käse but deducts a hundred marks a week for room and board. After all, it's in Jürgen's interest if Adolf's financial burdens are reduced and more money can be plowed back into the business. Herbert, too, has to turn over his apprentice's wages to the family and gets only an allowance.

By the time he is twenty, Jürgen has completely adapted himself to his parents' mode of life. He plans to take his master's license in a few years. At thirty-one, he'll take over his father's business. Until then, he is financially secure, has no responsibilities, and has time to cultivate his inner life.

He has gotten used to his parents' stormy relationship. As a child and even as an adolescent, he often used to cry when they quarreled. Almost all their fights involved the reaffirmation of Adolf's superiority.

Edith has no authority over the checking account Adolf maintains to take care of both household and business transactions. Edith writes out the checks. Adolf signs them.

She has no control either over the family's savings account or its small portfolio. If you let women get their hands on the money, they've got you at their mercy.

Edith argues that something could happen to him. He gets angry. She'll get his money soon enough.

He keeps implying that he has some money invested in mortgages. When Edith goes through his papers after his death, she finds there are only 4,600 marks in securities and 2,500 in the savings account.

"I wonder what he did with all that money," Edith says. "We made quite a bit during those years and allowed ourselves very little."

2 9   Adolf Schütrumpf dies in 1974 at the age of sixty, several months after the couple has celebrated their twenty-fifth anniversary. They still have the furniture that they bought during the first six years of their marriage. Only the curtains, wallpaper, and house plants have been replaced a few times. Even the kitchen dishes and some of the pots and pans date back to those first years.

The apartment is small. Seventy-nine square meters: entryway, bath, kitchen, pantry, living room, master bedroom and children's room, with only one door separating them.

At night the boys can hear their parents talking. Adolf's tirades sound like endless, monotonous prayers. He talks incessantly at Edith.

Edith's voice sounds nagging. She'd like some peace.

Herbert takes his parents' nocturnal arguments in his stride. The old man is all steamed up again tonight, he says.

The boys know what it's all about. The emptier the marriage gets, the greater the burden that is placed on sex to give it some semblance of meaning. Adolf is always especially eager for it on evenings that have been spent in petty quarreling. He needs some proof that they still love each other.

A man like Adolf does not live on in his works and has no history. He doesn't see the part he plays in history or recognize the contribution he makes to society. This is why he lives on only in his children and his children's children and in what little he can leave them.

Every successful sexual act confirms for him, potentially, the immortality he yearns for. Only in the sexual act can he realize himself fully, respect himself, demonstrate his unbroken masculinity. When he talks about this, he speaks of love and marriage. But Jürgen knows what these words really mean. They betray a man's need to possess a woman so that he will not despair of his own inadequacy, so that he will not sink into historical oblivion.

Adolf is still trying to prove his superiority. When company comes and he has had something to drink, he ridicules Edith and her little catastrophes. Once, when they were on vacation, she proudly served a piece of meat she had gotten at a bargain price. He could tell right away that it was horse meat.

He quite openly expresses his sorrow that she will die before he does and his fears of being left alone. He frequently talks about her frail health.

Edith suffers from allergies. There are a number of foods she can't eat. Several times during the last years of the marriage, she has to be rushed to the hospital in an ambulance. Her throat swells up unexpectedly. She is in danger of suffocating. Adolf makes a point of mentioning that he can't ever leave her alone. One day when he came home from work, he found her lying on the floor. She was gasping for breath and was already blue in the face. After Adolf's death, she stops having these attacks.

3 0   They argue over trivial matters. Edith can hardly recall anymore what their eternal squabbling was all about—whether it was something she had done wrong or shouldn't have done or didn't do, or something he had told her she should or shouldn't do or should do this way or not this way, and so on.

Adolf knows how to exploit her lethargy. He claims something needs to be done. She thinks it's unnecessary. There's no hurry. There's no need to do that. If she won't do it, he says, then he'll do it himself. Now she rises to the bait. He's trying to pressure her into it, she says. If she doesn't do it, he will, and then he'll complain that he has to do everything himself and that she always just lies around and takes life easy.

He constantly kept thinking up new chores for her. If she didn't jump to it, he'd start a fight.

Jürgen can't remember what he would call a real fight between his parents. Oh, yes, later, says Edith, in those last months. Yes, that's true, Jürgen admits. Everything went to hell then.

The year passes uneventfully without any great ups or downs. The Schütrumpfs hardly ever go out. Adolf spends a lot of time watching TV. He never misses a sports event. Woe be to Edith if she forgets to wake him up to watch the lottery drawing. From May to October, the Schütrumpfs spend a few hours in the evening in the garden behind the house, the way they used to in the good old days. Adolf raises lettuce, tomatoes, carrots, radishes, cabbage, and potatoes. The Schütrumpfs put up some of the produce for the winter. Edith sits on a bench and watches him.

They have company a few times each year. For all practical purposes, their circle of friends consists only of Uncle Erich and his wife, Hilde, and Uncle Hans and his wife, Anni. Neither couple is related to the Schütrumpfs, but when Jürgen and Herbert were children they called them uncle and aunt, and the names have stuck. Sometimes the Mehligs' daughter Ute comes, too.

Erich Schindewolf is two years younger than Adolf and grew up on a small farm in L., a village near K. He originally wanted to be a professional soldier. The end of the war put an end to those plans. He came back to L. and ran the farm, which his older brother Georg was supposed to take over.

Georg returns from a POW camp in 1955. He has aged prematurely and is ill. He can do only light work and soon marries a war widow who owns a textile business. In the sixties, when the competition from the department stores gets keener, he gives up the business and retires early. The Schütrumpf children call him uncle, too, but he rarely comes to visit.

3 1   Adolf and Erich get to know each other when Adolf is assigned to do some plumbing at Erich's place. Erich leaves his family's farm and moves to a new government-built farm outside the village. The tiny house looks like a cheap development house. The outbuildings with their asphalt siding are a blight on the landscape. After twenty years, the place looks hopelessly shabby and ready to be torn down.

In the mid-fifties, Erich buys a truck and hires out to building contractors in the area. After ten years, the truck is little more than junk. Erich spends all his savings on a new one, and he also has to take out a mortgage on five acres, a fifth of his land holdings.

Hilde comes from a good family. Until 1955, her parents dealt in building materials in W., a county seat near K. They build a little retirement house next to the Schindewolfs. Hilde is their only daughter. Bit by bit they pump their savings into Erich's farm for machinery, feed, and so on. The farm is a bottomless pit. Jürgen remembers Aunt Hilde's mother. She would always sit there, say very little, and act as if she didn't exist at all.

Hilde is seventeen when she gets pregnant. She would have had only one more year to go in the *Gymnasium*. The work on the farm changes her. She's up at five, makes Erich's breakfast (he often has to drive a long way to his jobs), feeds the animals, milks the cows, cleans out the stalls. By eight in the morning she's drenched in sweat and exhausted.

She and Edith share their disappointment over their misspent lives. Erich drinks too much. He sometimes spends up to a hundred marks in an evening or drives into K. late at night to drink with his friends in a bar.

He is a prominent figure in the village. He was mayor until the revision of the voting districts. He is fire chief, president of the glee club, and head deacon of the church. He is also president of two farmers' co-ops. He attends meetings several evenings a week. In the morning, he has to sleep off his hangover. During the day, he's out on the road. Hilde does the farm work, sits home alone in the evenings, feels like a servant woman.

Herbert is bored by the women's conversations when Adolf and Erich run down to the Gasthaus zur Mitte between coffee and supper to get a few bottles of beer. They come back a bit drunk two hours later. They are in high spirits, talk loudly, and complain about their dreary, sourpuss wives.

Jürgen is fascinated by what the women say. Hilde and Edith unknowingly confirm the conclusions he has reached himself. Life is senseless drudgery. Edith and Hilde are prisoners of a fate they did not choose. Things just worked out that way.

This gives him a sense of safety. All striving is in vain. Life is meaningful only in the past. Adolf and Edith once loved each other and decided to build a life together.

The farther back in the past Adolf's stories lie, and the harsher the struggle is, the more exciting his prospects for the future. In one of Adolf's accounts, he is an apprentice in a small village near K.

He sleeps in an attic that is unheated. He spends long, sleepless summer nights in ninety-degree heat. In the winter, the condensation from his breath freezes stiff on the edge of his quilt. God, what heat and what an icy wind, he says. His apprentices nod patiently.

.   .   .

The workday starts at five; in the winter at six. Long before the others are up, little Adolf builds a fire in the kitchen stove and puts on water for the ersatz coffee. By the time the workers arrive at seven, he has the fire going in the stove of the workshop. Long before the master arrives, he is at work loading the carts.

As a reward for doing these chores, he got an apple and an egg on Saturday. Even a journeyman's wages weren't enough to feed a family of four. But people were happy in those days, and when the year was over, nobody had gone hungry after all.

3 2   Uncle Hans—his last name is Mehlig—is a managing director at Fahlbush & Siebert, a factory with about six hundred employees that is located in N., just over the town line from K. Early in the war, his job in the personnel office at the plant is deemed essential to the war effort, and he is therefore not called up for military duty. He is commander of the local SA* unit in N., and he comes to work in uniform.

Fahlbusch & Siebert make use of foreign workers who are housed in a camp near K. The regulations governing the treatment of these foreign forced laborers are strict. The German workers are not allowed to give them anything to eat, even though the foreign workers' rations are inadequate.

Some Germans are moved to pity. They smuggle food to the foreigners. If Mehlig gets wind of it, he doesn't fool around. The foreigner gets sent back to the camp for good. The German winds up at the front.

Mehlig assumes personal responsibility for the morale of the foreign workers. He carries a switch with him when he goes through

*Sturmabteilung—TRANS.

the plant. If he sees a foreigner standing around idly or, worse
yet, sitting down, he sneaks up on him and lets him have it with
his whip.

One day he catches a foreigner looking for scraps of food in the
garbage cans in front of the canteen.

Mehlig asks the man what he's doing, screams at him, hits him in
the face, works himself into a fury, pounds with both fists until the
man is bleeding, knocks him down, and—now completely beside
himself in his bloodthirsty rage—starts stomping on the man.

Some of the workers who witness the scene retreat into one of
the shops. Later, an ambulance team comes to pick the man
up. At first the incident seems to have no consequences. Then
rumors begin to circulate in N. that Mehlig has killed a foreign
worker.

A few weeks later, Mehlig is drafted and sent to the front. The rumor
is that he was tried before a party tribunal and lost his positions in
the party and in the SA.

Hans and Adolf get to know each other through the black market.
Mehlig is trading on a large scale. It takes a while before Adolf finds
out what Mehlig is doing.

Mehlig reported back to Fahlbusch & Siebert after the war, but the
workers' council prevented him from being rehired. Until the early
fifties, a lot of workers' council members in K. are Communists. They
are the first to assume responsibility in the postwar years. Some of the
time, even the chairman of the workers' council at Siebert is a
Communist.

But old Siebert finds a way to make use of Mehlig anyhow. The plant
is short of everything from raw materials to cardboard and crates for
packing. Mehlig sells part of the plant's production on the black
market, takes foodstuffs as payment, trades these for cigarettes, coffee,
liquor, and other luxury items, which he then exchanges for the
materials the plant needs.

. . .

Mehlig later undergoes denazification. The commission is made up of an LDP* representative to the Bundestag, a building contractor, and a worker. It is just after the currency reform. Siebert is on the verge of expanding. The builder is interested in landing some contracts. The LDP representative seeks the support of influential citizens in town.

Siebert, who has married old Fahlbusch's only daughter, is a member of a respected family. Mehlig slips through the laxly administered denazification process practically unscathed. He is classified a Nazi sympathizer and gets away with a fine of only a few hundred marks.

In the late fifties, he will have a journalist in court for libel. The journalist wrote an article about Mehlig's mistreatment of the foreign worker. There are no witnesses except for a member of the ambulance crew who says that the man was still alive when the ambulance delivered him back to the camp. Nothing further is known about the man. The journalist is forced to publish a retraction and pay 5,000 marks in damages.

Jürgen doesn't hear this story until years later when he is working for Fahlbusch & Siebert and Fritz tells it to him. He asks Adolf about it. Is that true about Uncle Hans?
   Adolf indignantly denies the accusation.
   "Anybody who says that's true is dirt in my book."
   He wouldn't hear a bad word about his friends, Jürgen says.

3 3   Mehlig and Schütrumpf look just right together, like a dog and his master. Adolf is short, but he has a big head and a fat belly. It was his belly that didn't suit the rest of him, Edith says.
   He is proud of his belly and presents it to the world like a banner.

*Liberal-Demokratische Partei—TRANS.

His belly is the external sign of his male authority. You don't know what you're talking about, Adolf says. If some little skinny runt comes along, nobody takes him seriously.

Adolf's hair is thin. His hands and fingers are thick and swollen; his legs short and bowed. His right shoulder is somewhat lower than the left because of all the heavy work he did as a boy. Every year from the time he was twelve, his parents sent him to his mother's brother's farm during summer vacations. It's healthy for him, they said. Adolf had to go work in the fields from dawn till dusk.

His movements, his posture, and his walk, marked by heavy work, are almost clumsy. Adolf was a real worker, Edith says. He could work himself half to death.

He almost always sits at the table with his legs spread apart. His chair is at an angle. One leg is placed in front of the chair, the other alongside it. His arms look short. When he reaches for something on the table, he moves his torso forward at the same time. When he drives a car, you have the feeling that he can't negotiate sharp curves.

Uncle Hans is a head taller than he is. He has thick coal-black hair that he combs straight back, bushy eyebrows, alert eyes, broad shoulders, and a solid body. His excess weight is better distributed than Adolf's. He stands very straight. Only the gestures he makes with his hands and arms have something artificial about them.

His suits look new and are always in flawless condition, while Adolf always looks as if he slept in his clothes. Adolf's suits don't fit him properly anywhere. They're baggy in one place and too tight in another. Mehlig's suits fit him to a T. Adolf prefers sporty flannel shirts. Uncle Hans wears white shirts with a bow tie.

Adolf is a Social Democrat because that's what his family has always been. Mehlig is the very image of the master race. Whatever Mehlig says is indisputable. He emphasizes the unquestionable truth of his statements by speaking in the plural.

"We've never let politics interfere with our friendship, have we, Adolf?" Adolf nods. Their relationship has always been based on a purely personal liking for each other.

Whenever Mehlig says "we," disagreement is out of the question. If he says "I" or "you," Adolf feels rebuffed. A painful distance opens up between him and Hans, and he quickly tries to bridge it again by saying something Mehlig will approve of. If Mehlig feels like baiting him, he turns Adolf's attempt at reconciliation away and contradicts what Adolf has said. Adolf is mystified. But I've heard you say that yourself, Hans.

These little misunderstandings amount to nothing more than a game. Mehlig and Schütrumpf need each other. Neither one of them has any friends. The relationship with Uncle Hans grows out of Adolf's admiration for his social superiors and out of his need to subjugate himself to someone stronger. The meaning and consequences of this subjugation are clear to both parties.

3 4   And Uncle Hans values the painful feelings that his friendship with Adolf evokes. Every visit to the Schütrumpfs is a kind of self-punishment because he is associating with people below him.

"What in the world was that nondescript salad that Edith served?" he asks his wife on the way home. Herring salad, Anni replies impassively.

Whenever Hans Mehlig invites the Schütrumpfs to his house in the suburbs, he feels he is degrading himself. Every time Adolf comes out of the bathroom, he sings the praises of the plumbing he installed twenty years ago. This speech is as sure to come as night is to follow day. Mehlig, with a pained expression on his face, agrees. When the Schütrumpfs leave, he airs out the house.

But still the friendship with Adolf gives him a feeling of self-satisfaction. It stands as proof that human ties mean more to him than social and economic differences. When he is with his friends in the party and with business colleagues, he boasts of this friendship. Believe me, he says, I know the worries and cares of the man in the street. I'm friends with a man who has a small plumbing business.

The ladies get along together well, too. In her conversations with Hilde Schindewolf, Edith plays the fellow sufferer whose husband oppresses her and does not appreciate her. With Anni Mehlig, she plays the mother and keeper of the hearth, the one who holds all the invisible threads of family life firmly in her hand.

Let the men think they are the masters of the household. She and Anni Mehlig know that their husbands need them.

When she talks with Anni, she sees Adolf in a different light. The boorish roughneck turns into a sensitive man who is in need of love and relies on his wife for support. Edith even pulls out his intellectual accomplishments again, though they have long since proved to be spurious.

The difference in their husbands' social status melts away. It no longer matters that Mehlig runs a plant with six hundred employees and has almost godlike power, while Adolf employs only two young workers and an apprentice. A man is a man.

Here the two sexes see eye to eye. A woman is a woman.

That's what Uncle Hans and Adolf say when they talk about their wives. Wilhelmine Siebert, Siebert's widow and the old heiress to Fahlbusch & Siebert, is the only exception. She is a lady.

When Edith and Anni meet at the Mehligs' for coffee (it's so much more comfortable there), their conversation shows how totally the men dominate the women's consciousnesses. Their talk turns exclusively around the men, their work, their behavior, and their problems.

. . .

Jürgen and Herbert are sometimes allowed to go along. You can play with Ute.

Later, when Jürgen has finished his apprenticeship, Adolf drops occasional hints. A nice girl, that Ute. That's the kind of daughter-in-law I'd like to have if one of you boys gets married someday. It is taken for granted that Jürgen and Herbert will marry.

I always considered my parents' marriage a model of what a marriage should be, Jürgen says.

Ute is out of the question. She has one leg that is shorter than the other, and she had to go to a special school. She's studying home economics and doing a practicum in a nursing home.

With Anni, Edith can talk about other men, too. Once a month, they go to the Café Specht in the afternoon. They both still have their looks. They discuss their physical attractiveness with pride. They're both a little plump, but there's nothing flabby about them. Other men appreciate that, even if their own husbands don't.

Anni sets the standard for Edith. Bit by bit, Adolf has to outfit her in the same style as Anni, only cheaper.

But just as good, he stresses.

Sometimes he gives Edith jewelry, too. We couldn't keep up with the Mehligs in that line, of course, Edith says.

But that wasn't at all necessary. That was a lovely relationship between the Mehligs and us. Money wasn't important in it at all.

3 5   After completing his apprenticeship, Jürgen works for his father from the fall of 1969 until the spring of 1974. It is a quiet, unproblematic time. His previous experience has taught him that it doesn't pay to have great ambitions. He once saw a photograph of the composer Maurice Ravel in a book. Ravel was wearing ordinary street clothes and leaning against a piano. He had a cigarette in his mouth.

.   .   .

A composer who wears everyday clothes and smokes a cigarette. An ordinary person. The banality of life on all social and cultural levels confuses him.

In the end, he comes to accept Adolf's view of life. No one should reach for the stars. Everyone should stay in the place where fate has put him.

All a man needs is a warm home, enough to eat, tolerable work, and a nice wife. Jürgen is glad not to have any responsibility. He does his work, pays his room and board, and is left in peace. He makes a point of not thinking about himself. Only in recent months has he begun to think about why everything happened the way it did.

As late as the summer of 1974, he says to his friend Freddy: "I don't even want to know who I really am. I don't want to know what's inside me. I bet that if people could see inside themselves they'd be shocked.

"I bet that there's a terrible mess inside me."

It's all he can do to get through the four weeks a year when he has to run the business. That's when Adolf and Edith go on vacation.

They take a vacation for the first time in their lives when Jürgen is in the third year of his apprenticeship. Adolf explains in great detail what is to be done, which jobs should be started, how much to pay the worker and Käse, which bills should be paid, who all might call up.

Reluctantly, he decides to give Jürgen the authority to sign checks for four weeks.

Jürgen enjoys being alone, having the apartment to himself, working without his father, being able to make his own schedule. There's no Adolf to stomp through the boys' room in the morning and yell: "Roll out, you old booze hound."

Adolf is just kidding, but Jürgen doesn't like it anyhow.

Jürgen sometimes turns up a half hour late for work, quits early, or takes a longer break, all under the pretense that he has to see customers. He can rely on Käse. In small businesses, the employees work like demons. The workers criticize the boss behind his back for being lazy or letting things slip, and they laugh at his admonitions.

No meals to be eaten the instant they're served up. Nobody to fuss at him if he goes out in the evening: I won't be able to pry you out of bed in the morning!

The only thing he doesn't like is dealing with customers. They don't take him seriously. In the fall of 1975, when we have our talks for this book, Jürgen is twenty-six, but he still looks twenty.

Jürgen is happy to leave the business end of things to his father. He has no desire for a business of his own as long as Adolf is willing to carry on. If he'd never had that liver trouble, Jürgen says, none of this would have happened. The thing Jürgen had always feared most was his father's death.

He would often imagine that his father had died. He would start crying at his father's deathbed, and his father would have to console him. Perhaps he imagined his father's death so often just so he could imagine his father consoling him.

Every time he pictured his father's death, the pain was overwhelming. He often sat in his room with tears streaming down his face. Whenever he heard of a death, or saw on TV that someone had died, he would instantly remember that his father would have to die sometime, too, and he would begin to cry. He was embarrassed if someone saw him like this. He never told anyone why he was crying. Usually he was able to get away from other people in time.

He enjoyed being alone, but he feared his father's death.

I ask him how he pictured the time after his father's death. He hesitates. I never really thought about that, he says.

3 6   When the Schütrumpfs come home from their vacation, everything is in order. The workshop is still standing; all the work scheduled has been completed; no customers have deserted them. But Adolf complains anyhow.

A man like Adolf is unable to face the fact that the world can go on without him. The only successes he recognizes are his own. He blames other people for his failures. In his view, the function of criticism is to improve other people's performance. Since his own performance admits of no further improvement, he is unreceptive to criticism.

But in spite of this the Schütrumpfs take several weeks off every summer for the next four years. These annual trips seem to open new dimensions of life and experience for them.

All of a sudden my folks developed a new independence, Jürgen says. I was really surprised that they were able to break out of their routine for a few weeks every year.

They travel through half of Europe. Their favorite destinations are the places Adolf got to know during the war. Their trips are journeys into the past that bring alive again the stories he had told in the first years of their marriage. The boyish enthusiasm with which he shows Edith the streets and squares, the cities and landscapes he came to know in his youth, is infectious.

His pride amuses her. He acts as if he had been the first to discover Amsterdam and Brussels, Paris and Naples. He leads her through the streets with an air of mystery. He suddenly stops in front of a restaurant, a café, a hotel, or a tailor's shop.

It is the restaurant he told her about almost twenty-five years ago, the one where he had often eaten when he was a soldier. It's the hotel where I went with that cute little girl I once told you about. That's the tailor who made the pants I was still wearing in 1947.

· · ·

What Adolf likes most is to visit places where he once knew people. In his stories, he often mentioned the good relationships he, a simple foot soldier, established with local people during the war.

Suddenly these stories take on reality. It was possible then, despite the hatred and ideology that were handed down from above, to see each other as human beings with much in common.

It is often hard for Adolf to recognize old acquaintances. Skinny men in baggy uniforms or suits are now potbellied types who can't fit into their clothes. Sturdy middle-aged men have become tottering grandpas. A face that was once striking has given way to pig's eyes and dangling jowls.

Adolf and Edith find themselves sitting at a table with total strangers. They try to overcome the language barrier by talking loud and using their hands. There's no need to dig up the past again. There are good and bad people everywhere in the world.

Adolf is good. A man like him can strike up acquaintances anywhere, people he can get along with and help, people who will in turn help him. He and his kind know what counts in life. What they have learned can be put to good use anywhere. It's true all over the world, with slight variations. They make up the International of the common man. They are at home anywhere because they know one thing for sure: There's no place like home.

Edith is amazed at the way Adolf responds to a hospitality that is foreign to her. All at once he is wearing a beret, drinking red wine instead of beer and schnapps. In his fishing gear, he looks like the natives, and his portliness takes on some of their bourgeois peasant solidity.

He refuses to acknowledge that any language barriers exist. He won't resort to phrase books or dictionaries. He points to people and objects, talks with his hands and his face, develops pantomimic skills, and makes all verbal communication appear superfluous.

·   ·   ·

Edith never gets a chance to make use of the linguistic knowledge she has picked up in adult-education courses. Adolf is quicker and gets what he wants.

3 7   Adolf's trips have a childlike and adventuresome quality to them. Weeks before, he puts up the tent in the yard and looks at it for hours at a time with a case of beer next to his chair. Is something wrong with the tent? Edith asks. Leave me alone, he says.

The next day, the tent is flat on the ground. Adolf saws up the metal poles, welds them together differently, sews panels of canvas. Next he welds hooks and eyes onto the back of the trailer, pads the luggage rack with foam rubber, hangs curtains on the rear windows.

Adolf sweats and swears, is nervous, hurts himself, but refuses to let anyone bandage his cut. He curses out his sons, who are never there to lend a hand when he needs them, and scolds Edith, who is always doing things wrong.

If I find the hammer, I'll bust your head with it. Fortunately he doesn't find the hammer in the chaos around him.

Finally he's finished. The tent is attached directly to the rear of the trailer. They'll sleep in the car. The living room now opens onto a spacious porch with side walls.

Then Adolf goes shopping. When they leave, they'll have food enough for six weeks, a complete set of kitchen utensils, fishing gear, a portable TV that runs off a battery, and enough furniture for four people.

All of Adolf's trips are journeys to disaster. In his frantic preparations for departure, he leaves his traveler's checks in the sideboard, and when he first sets up the tent he finds a crucial pole missing.

He often gets lost. Edith, who is supposed to keep track of their course on the map, never knows where they are.

Every wrong turn he makes and every red light he runs is cause for argument. Adolf drives like a man possessed. All he cares about is covering distance.

He doesn't even take time out to pee, Edith says. He drives hundreds of kilometers without stopping.

When they finally arrive at a campground, driver and passenger stagger out of the car. Their circulation is about to quit on them.

Now the drama of setting up the tent begins. It was usually dark by then, Edith says.

The next argument is inevitable.

A major source of conflict was that Adolf could not leave well enough alone with the tent. He kept on fiddling with it through their whole vacation. The slightest breeze had him reinforcing the side poles. If there was a threat of rain, he started digging a drainage ditch around the tent.

Everybody else put up their tents in five minutes and never touched them again for three weeks. We were at work on ours the whole time.

They were always worn out when they left and worn out when they came back, Jürgen says. But then they fed off their trip for the rest of the year. Always the same stories. The time when a deer ran into the car, the time when a buzzard crashed through the windshield when they were doing seventy-five mph on the autobahn.

That idiot cop in Geneva who signaled Adolf to make an illegal turn and then fined him thirty francs to boot, and the time they met the goalie from the Bavaria Munich soccer team at that campground on the Bay of Biscay. Whenever they told these stories, Jürgen says, they even picked up old arguments where they had left off. Was it his fault or hers that they took the wrong turn in Caserta?

3 8 In 1970, just before he turns twenty-one, Jürgen is allowed to take his first vacation trip. He takes a group tour to the Adriatic. Most of the group on the bus is made up of couples of all different ages. There are three or four men traveling alone and a few women and girls who are in pairs. Jürgen is disappointed that there are no nice girls.

The resort town is a disappointment, too. Several rows of ugly concrete buildings line the beach for miles on end, a sprawling city that lives entirely off the tourist trade and consists of nothing but hotels and shops. It's hard to imagine that real people lived here thirty years ago.

But Jürgen soon finds himself fascinated with the place. He notes with interest everything that is different from home: the different smells that come from the kitchen of his pension, the different food, the different tastes, the different way of furnishing a room, the different merchandise in the stores, the different drinks in the bars, the different cars, the different stench of gasoline, the different people.

In the morning he goes swimming. In the afternoon he travels along the coast in a bus. On his second day, he discovers a village with a little harbor on a rocky stretch of coast. It could have been a fishing village in the past. It still has some old houses. The men who are fixing up the boats are in their undershirts. Jürgen takes off his shirt and sits on the harbor wall. The tourists probably think he is a native.

He dreams about coming here to stay, finding some kind of job, living a simple life, leaving everything behind that's waiting for him in N.: his job, the people, Edith and Adolf. He'll start all over again, marry a girl, maybe the waitress in the Miramar.

.   .   .

After a while he discovers two or three other older towns at some distance from the tourist beaches. He enjoys the bustle in the narrow streets; the many little stores and artisans' workshops; the small cars that wend their way between the pedestrians, the stands in front of the shops, and the chairs in front of the cafés; the three-wheeled vehicles that the tradesmen and small shopkeepers use to transport their tools and wares.

He found himself wondering, he says, just what the difference was between a plumber's shop there and his father's three-man business in N. He couldn't see any great difference. Still, he would rather have been born a plumber down there.

What he enjoyed most was being on the main streets after five in the afternoon. At first he had been amazed at the number of people and thought there must be a meeting or some other special event on. But then the people just kept walking aimlessly up and down the streets in twos and threes. Old ones and young ones, mostly men. Imagine if people did that here. Once a day, all the people leave their houses to go walking on the streets and meet each other. For two hours, the main street in town was crowded with people, and nobody driving a car seemed to mind at all.

Why can't Germans be like that? Jürgen asks.
   The people were much nicer to their children, too. The dogs were much better tempered, and the people had more time for themselves. They talked to each other more, and they could sit in front of the cafés for hours without eating or drinking anything, and no waiter would ever think of asking them to leave. At night especially they sat outside on the streets. It was different in the tourist centers. People worked much more there. That was the German influence.

3 9   Jürgen has his meals at the same table with a young man and two young women. The man talks endlessly about the nightclubs he has explored, where they have the best band, and what the prices are

like. In the evening, Jürgen goes to one of these bars. It's a discothèque. It has a front room and another one behind for dancing.

There is a long bar in the front room. On the wall across from the bar there are little booths with low upholstered seats and small tables. The larger room has these low couches in it, too, arranged in clusters. The dance floor is small.

Jürgen feels out of place. The women look sophisticated to him, the men elegant. Everybody is very sure of himself. Nobody seems to feel lonely. The crowd looks like one big family.

The happiness that these people share makes Jürgen feel he doesn't belong. He doesn't know anyone. The idea of going up to a girl and talking to her is inconceivable to him. Many of the girls seem to be local. He stands at the bar and orders a beer. The waiter speaks German.

While he's drinking his beer, someone tugs at his sleeve. It's one of the women from his table at the pension. She has a gorgeous man with her, slim, dark, black-haired. He's wearing white slacks, a black shirt open at the front, a green velvet jacket. The shirt and jacket are tapered at the waist. He wears a fine chain around his neck.
   Jürgen has bought new clothes for the trip. He's wearing light-colored slacks and a dark blue blazer with gold buttons. The sight of this man knocks him for a loop. He feels shabby and second-rate by comparison.

You look very elegant, the woman says. Would you like to dance with me? Stunned, Jürgen nods. She waves to her handsome companion and pulls Jürgen out onto the dance floor. I just didn't know what to make of it, Jürgen says. Next to that guy I looked like a post office clerk.

That's an expression Adolf uses. When he was young, the boys working at the post office always had just enough money to afford a cigarette and to show off with it whenever they came into a place. They thought they were better than boys apprenticing in the trades.

Jürgen is a terrible dancer. When he was a boy, he once went to a fair in Uncle Erich's village and danced with Aunt Hilde and with his mother, who taught him a few steps. He danced a few times in N., too, at his graduation party and at a carnival ball the Tuspo 96 held. When he was drunk, he could dance just fine.

The woman's name is Heidrun. She puts her arms around his neck and pulls him in close to her. The men dance with both hands on the women's backs, almost down onto their rumps. All the couples dance very close. Jürgen and his partner do, too. They take tiny steps. He can feel her breasts. Her firm thighs press against his. The dance floor is crowded. A man dancing near them has one arm tucked in between his partner and himself. His hand is on the woman's breast. He is moving his thumb back and forth and seems to be stroking her nipple. Jürgen looks away quickly, but he has to look back several times.

Jürgen and Heidrun go back to the bar. The handsome man is gone, but another, even more handsome one turns up in his place. Heidrun lets him talk to her. Jürgen prepares himself to be deserted, but she turns back to him and leaves the other man standing there.

During the next dance, Jürgen's hand creeps onto her breast. She has huge breasts. When his thumb is on her nipple, his fingers can just barely span the outer side of her breast. His penis starts to throb. Her eyes look different now. Hungry, Jürgen says. She brushes her lips across his twice. Then she opens her mouth, places it over his, and thrusts her thick tongue between his lips. Jürgen opens his mouth and sticks his tongue into her mouth, too. Thirty seconds later, he has an ejaculation and feels the dampness in his pant leg.

Come on, let's go, she says.

4 0   The first time Jürgen has sexual intercourse without paying for it is a disgusting experience of indescribable delight. He is often on the verge of shoving her aside and running away. Then he throws himself on her again with greater ferocity than before.

For a while, they make love with her on her back. Suddenly she pushes him away, runs her tongue over his chest and belly, and takes his penis into her mouth. It takes him a moment to realize what she is doing. Then he tries to get away from her. She follows him with her head, moaning with pleasure. He grabs her hair and tries to pull her away. Don't, he stammers, don't.

She lets go of his penis, brings her face up to his, and kisses him. Her kiss tasted sour somehow; he doesn't quite know how to describe it. He was disgusted and almost had to vomit. But then she lay down on her back again, and it was indescribably beautiful.

Later she frightened him again. When he was lying on his back, she straddled him and ran his penis deep inside her.
   "I wouldn't have thought anything like that was possible," he says. "She was like a fury. She treated me like a machine. I think all she was interested in was satisfying herself."

Heidrun is married. Her husband is a butcher and cattle dealer who has a big butcher shop in the north end. They always take separate vacations so they won't have to close the place down. The building the shop is in, a new six-story structure with eighteen apartments, belongs to them. They also own three older buildings in other parts of the city, all of them apartment houses.

Heidrun is twenty-four; her husband is thirty. They have been married five years. He took over the buildings and the business from his parents, who are both still alive. She apprenticed with him in the shop.

. . .

Jürgen and Heidrun spend the rest of their vacation together. He shows her the villages he has discovered. They get along well. His fears and inhibitions don't seem to bother her. He tells her about his attempts to write music, his dreams of becoming a composer or conductor, his ridiculous belief that he was a great philosopher. He has suddenly developed some self-irony. Only in bed at night does he feel she's too much for him. He can't bring himself to tell her that.

She was always fun and in a good mood, Jürgen says. But not blasé or conceited like some girls. But in bed she was a madwoman. She could never get enough. Sometimes when we were making love, she would keep saying "Yes" for five or ten minutes at a time, nothing but "Yes," louder and louder until she was almost screaming and I had to put my hand over her mouth.

On the trip home, she sits next to her girl friend again. On the overnight stop, Jürgen shares a room with an older man. During their last meal together, he asks her if they can meet sometime in K. She doesn't want to.

He checks out all the butcher shops in the north end, one after another. No luck. One day he is working in the north end. Jürgen buys a little hamburger for his morning break. The butcher is working at his block. A young woman serves Jürgen. When he gives her his order, the other salesgirl in the shop stares at him, turns quickly away, and disappears into the refrigerator room. As she is pulling the door shut behind her, he realizes that it is Heidrun. He almost didn't recognize her.

He didn't make any further attempts to meet her after that.

4 1   Work is devoid of meaning for Jürgen during these years. It is an unpleasant but inevitable part of life that it's best not to talk about.

If anyone asks him what kind of work he does or what his job is, he answers: "Who cares?"

Life begins once work is over. Käse starts off his morning every day with a little ritual saying. Get out of the way, work! he says. Here we come.

The day is spent waiting for quitting time; the week in waiting for the weekend; the year in waiting for vacation.

As soon as work is over, the race with time begins. It doesn't matter what you do, Jürgen says. You always waste your time. You're so afraid of wasting the little bit of time you have that you do all kinds of stupid things.

On two workday evenings, he takes a bath after supper and goes straight to bed. On those nights, he gets all the sleep he can. Jürgen saw somebody in a film version of a Maupassant story do this. He admires Maupassant a lot.

He likes Gregor von Rezzori, too. He finds Peter Handke quite good but too boring. Günter Grass is more an author for older upper-class ladies. But Albert Camus is really good. He describes the dead-end quality of human life.

When he doesn't go to bed early, he goes out. He hasn't touched his piano for ages. His music lies buried under his schoolbooks in the closet where the wood lice are making themselves at home in it and in his old diaries, too.

Zarathustra and Ernst Jünger's *Storm of Steel* stand untouched among the twenty or thirty ex-best sellers that make up Edith's library: *The Forests Sing Forever, Via Mala, The Citadel, The Spy Who Came In from the Cold, The Women of the House of Wu, How Tender Was Suleyken, Teeming Tropics, Like a Teardrop in the Ocean.*

Jürgen spends a lot of time with a certain Uwe Hühnerfuss, who was in Pels's class. Hühnerfuss dropped out of school, learned show-window decorating, and is studying set design at the art school. He paints abstract pictures with human figures hidden in them.

Jürgen meets a few art students and artists through Uwe. Their manner puts him off.

I wouldn't say that they were rude, but they acted as if everything were a matter of course.

When he goes to one of their apartments for the first time, they are sitting on sofas and chairs in a circle. Some are sitting on the floor. There are two cases of beer next to the wall.

When he asks if he can have a bottle, someone says: "Just cut the talk and take one."

They talk constantly, but he understands very little. Sometimes when he thinks he has something to contribute, they shut him up.

"Everybody knows that already. That has nothing to do with what we're talking about. God, you talk a lot of nonsense."

Jürgen has the feeling that behind the coldness of the world as he knows it, he has discovered a new world that no one is aware of. You wouldn't believe the kind of problems they had.

He felt he was an idiot who had wasted his time with the wrong things from the very beginning. Whenever he told about a story he had read by Maupassant, they smiled condescendingly. Here, read something worthwhile for once.

They are alien creatures for him. They had a totally different lifestyle, he says.

There are people who get up whenever they please, do work they enjoy, and live anyway they like. They're different from my kind.

He vacillates between admiration and rejection. It's nice if you can live that way, but what if everybody did it? Everything would collapse.

In their apartments he misses the kind of order he is used to at home.

The kitchens and bedrooms were always the messiest. The sink would be full of dirty dishes from the last three days, and they hadn't taken out the garbage for at least a week.

"I couldn't have lived in that kind of mess. Maybe I could now."

He doesn't like their clothes either. I couldn't run around looking so sloppy.

4 2   When Jürgen goes into a bar or gets together with his new friends, he changes his manner. His voice takes on a different tone. When he tells a story, he keeps having to laugh at what he's relating even though everyone else remains serious.

When he listens to someone else, he cocks his head to one side. When he starts to speak, he makes strange movements with his head. While he's talking, his hands and arms are in perpetual motion.

A local TV station films a bar frequented by students and artists. Most of these artists have not been working artists for a long time. They earn their living as art teachers, but they still act as if they were artists.

The cameraman films the table where Jürgen and his friends are sitting. When Jürgen sees the film on TV, he doesn't recognize himself. It's disgusting how I look in that film.

His favorite bars now are the ones where students and artists go. Even in K., many foreign bars open during these years. Local people hardly ever visit them. There are two big hippie bars where dealers in hash and other stuff operate.

Wearing his suits and sports jackets from Brenninkmeier's men's department, he struts through the bars like a picture-book English lord through the jungles of central Africa. He has on a shirt Edith has ironed to perfection, and a bow tie. He carries an umbrella in his hand. The seedier the bar is, the more he plays the gentleman out to do a little slumming. He signals to the waiter with a mannered wave of his hand.

. . .

He orders his drink in overly elaborate language. One of his models is Jack Nicholson in *Easy Rider*, the alcoholic, no-good son of a wealthy family. He makes no concessions to the dress code of the modest subculture of K. A few times, someone offers him a drag on a joint. He shows no anger but simply declines with a grand gesture.

Uwe and Jürgen drink a lot whenever they get together. They talk for hours and get drunker and drunker. In an affected voice, Jürgen constructs endless complex sentences, loses track of his antecedents, weaves absurd verbal fabrics that have less and less to do with the thoughts he wants to convey the more impenetrable their structure grows and the more reckless he becomes in losing sentence elements.

Uwe responds in slowly enunciated words and in brief sentences that are not marked by any punctuation and that degenerate into mere babbling in the course of the evening.

He likes to speak in obscure metaphors. He can't express a thought, describe a fact, or outline a position without resorting to elaborate figures of speech. His metaphors gradually lose their points of reference and become sibylline pronouncements that seem devoid of meaning.

When unfathomable grammatical constructions and purely metaphorical metaphors have brought them to the point where comprehension has become virtually impossible, Uwe and Jürgen understand each other best. Deeply moved, they fall into each other's arms, kiss, and feel they are on the verge of illuminating the mysteries of life.

The only difference was that I had to get up at six-thirty the next morning while he slept till noon. But I don't need much sleep.

Sometimes I don't get more than three or four hours' sleep for three nights in a row.

4 3   Jürgen is proud of his friendship with Uwe. Uwe provides endless material for conversation. Whenever a few artist types or hangers-on from the art world get together, they tell stories about him. They can talk about him for whole evenings at a time.

There was the time he stood on the roof and peed through the studio skylight onto Professor B.'s head, prompting the professor to say: I think it's raining. Would someone please close the skylight?

The time he started a fight in a bar and the owner called the police and there was a god-awful brawl and everybody ended up getting arrested except Uwe.

The stories everyone likes best are the ones about Uwe's inexhaustible ingenuity in doing people out of their money.

Uwe visits a friend. He is drunk and brings two drunken friends with him. One of them falls asleep instantly. The other turns ugly and threatens to smash up the apartment. Uwe looks on with a mild and understanding expression on his face. He says no one should take his rowdy friend seriously. The fellow just has an aversion for certain styles of décor.

The host smiles guiltily. The rowdy is roaming through the apartment with a wild look on his face. The host follows him nervously. Later, Uwe makes a phone call. He picks up the receiver, dials, and waits for the other party to answer. In the meantime he says politely: I hope this is all right?

The host nods unhappily. As long as you're not calling New York.

"Just Munich," Uwe says.

Speaking in elaborate and obscure riddles, he makes the party in Munich guess who he is. It takes several minutes for the Munich party to establish Uwe's identity. The host stands by resigned, imagining what his telephone bill will be.

. . .

Uwe finally comes to the point. He needs at least two hundred marks. He and his two friends are out on a binge. The bar owners won't give an inch. They want cash on the barrel. In the last twenty-four hours, he and his friends have been able to worm their way out of bars twice when they didn't have enough money to pay the check.

At lunchtime he had managed to locate a noble soul who had stood them to three Jägerschnitzel. He, Uwe, had used the direct approach, a tried and true method.

"Sir, you see before you three worthy gentlemen who would not refuse your invitation to a modest meal."

The man had shown great sensitivity in the area of liquid refreshment, too. All it had taken was a simple request.

"May we make so bold as to ask for three beers as well?" Later, the philanthropist volunteered without even being asked: "Three more beers, gentlemen?"

He, Uwe, presented the man with a signed sketch on a paper napkin.

The celebration is progressing into its third night. The party in Munich seems to be sympathetic. He agrees to cable some money immediately. Uwe gives him the address of the apartment he is in at the moment. What's your street and house number here?

Uwe can't be expected to know things like that. His orientation in town is purely visual. He refuses to carry an address book. He sometimes drags Jürgen around some part of town for a whole evening looking for the house where a good friend of his lives. He finally ends up ringing just any old doorbell. He has sure instincts for this kind of thing. The people prove hospitable and have plenty to drink on hand.

On the evening in question here, a period of waiting begins. Uwe indicates to his host that some beer would be welcome. He refuses to send the rowdy for beer and appeals to his host's insight into human nature. His crew is exhausted. As Uwe puts it: It's a matter of the bull's-eye in repose as against the mobility of the elbow.

The host gets the point. He is the elbow. No one can expect Uwe to fetch his own beer. And he who pays fetches. When the host returns, he finds that no disasters have occurred in his absence. He is relieved.

Later, Uwe starts dancing with the rowdy. The host carries vases, the TV, the record player, and the glass coffee table to safety. But Uwe and the rowdy fall against a freestanding bookcase. Uwe foils all attempts at putting the books back by building bizarre sculptures out of them.

The host suggests calling up the post office to find out how long it takes to wire money from Munich. The information they receive is reassuring. Uwe and the rowdy start to cook goulash and dumplings in the host's kitchen. The rowdy turns out to be an Upper Bavarian expert on dumplings. Uwe discovers his host's wine.

The smells from the kitchen wake up the third man. It is Jürgen. Uwe tells him that a lovely party is in progress. Jürgen restores his English appearance. Uwe and the rowdy look like two faded and tattered parrots.

After their meal, the gentlemen stretch out in armchairs. The host presses them to leave. You have to go now. I have work to do.

Uwe meditates. His words roll out of his mouth like potato dumplings.

The rowdy wants to get out of this stupid pad. All this *Better-Homes-and-Gardens* décor makes him puke. He feels as if he's in the show window of a furniture store. Uwe is willing to make concessions: We could go to a friendly neighborhood bar until the green turns up. Do you have any money left, Jürgen?

Jürgen's spirits are low. These three days have taken their toll on his inner reserves, but his principles remain intact. People like Uwe belong in a work camp. They sponge from other people and have a fine time doing it. Thieves. Crooks. But lack of sleep and too much alcohol rob Jürgen of his will. He doesn't have the strength to stick to his principles.

And he doesn't know what's going on. Uwe placates him, saying that the two hundred marks will be coming any moment now.
"What two hundred marks?"
"Don't worry about it."

The host sees his chance. I could lend you a hundred marks, and you can come back here tomorrow and get the rest. Uwe refuses indignantly: That would be a terrible imposition on you!
Besides, he's expecting two hundred.
"Then give me the money," the rowdy says in a rage. "I want out of this dump."
Uwe yields. If his friends want to leave, then he will leave, too. The host, much relieved, pulls a hundred marks out of his wallet.

Days later, Jürgen runs into the host. The money from Munich still hasn't arrived. The whole affair is embarrassing to Jürgen. He calls Uwe to account about it. Uwe pretends he can't remember. Eventually, the injured host calms down, too.
When people start talking about Uwe now, Jürgen can tell a story or two himself.

4 4   Jürgen's friendship with Uwe has the kind of importance for him that his friendship with Pels had several years earlier.
The only friends I've ever had have been men, he says now. I've always been after women, but what I've really wanted from them I've never gotten.
What does a little bit of screwing amount to? I've never had a real friendship with a woman.

But Jürgen suffers under a delusion. He thinks Uwe lived a life of complete freedom. It was Uwe who showed him how vapid a normal life was.

He feels that Uwe's way of life constantly called his own into question. We all let ourselves be pushed around, he says. We're dumb enough to fall for that line about what would happen if everybody lived like that. Everybody has to go his own way. He feels he has never been able to do that and has realized it too late.

Jürgen could never bring himself to be as radical and daring as Uwe. Uwe makes a principle of riding the trolley without a ticket. Whatever he needs in the way of food and drink, he steals from supermarkets. Uwe is a star shoplifter.

He steals things a couple of times when Jürgen is with him. Before he pockets something, he shows Jürgen what he's got. Jürgen goes into instant panic. He can't think straight to save himself. He's scared out of his wits. He begins to sweat and stink. He wants to run away. But on the other hand he doesn't want to leave Uwe in the lurch. He goes out of the store and waits on the next street corner. Uwe usually steals gourmet foods and expensive liquor.

It embarrasses Jürgen, too, when Uwe approaches strangers on the street and asks them for money or a cigarette. Jürgen walks on as if he doesn't know Uwe. He is particularly ill at ease when Uwe accosts women.

Uwe will approach any and all women he sees. Would they like to come along to the Copabianca or the Valencia? Sometimes he invites them to his place. He and his friend are putting on a big party.

"Hey, Jürgen, tell them it's true. We're going to have a big party, right?"

Sometimes the girls join them. Jürgen struts along a bit to one side and doesn't know what to say. Sometimes he blurts out some inane remark or another: You remind me of a character in a Zola novel. He has never read Zola, but he knows that Zola was a French writer.

Or he'll say: You have to assume that everything that lives in the desert is dangerous. Take me, for example. A minute ago I was lonely. Now we're walking side by side.

If the girls hesitate, Uwe turns on his powers of persuasion. Jürgen tries to stop him from this: Come on, Uwe. Let's go.

One time when Uwe picks up a girl, she seems more interested in Jurgen. Up in his room, Uwe plays the artist and starts painting something. Jürgen and the girl hit it off. He immediately puts aside his affectations and talks like a normal human being.

Uwe signals to him that he should stop fooling around and move in for the attack. Jürgen caresses her arm. He runs his fingernails up and down her arm, hoping this will excite her. After a while her skin is all red and scratched up.

Uwe butts in. Here's where you take hold, you amateur. He grabs at her crotch.
She slaps him. Uwe yells at her and leaves.

Would you like to sleep with me? the girl asks.
They begin with the girl on her back. Then Jürgen starts trying different positions. He runs through the whole repertoire he had learned with Heidrun.
The girl stands up. Either you sleep with me the right way or not at all. I don't like all this fooling around.

Jürgen is completely taken aback. He tries again in the normal position, but he's lost his erection.
"Well, that's that," the girl says. "Shall we go have a beer?"

After they've had one beer together, Jürgen gets up to leave.
I have to get home. When he gets there, he masturbates and imagines doing everything with her that she wouldn't let him do.

4 5   Once or twice a week, he goes to one of the few gay bars in K.

In this respect, too, K. is a provincial town. There are none of those fancy baroque places you can find in the big cities. These local bars are not noticeably different from the ones heterosexuals frequent.

The clientele is lower middle class and conventional-looking. They make a point of being conservative and respectable in appearance. Hardly any of them would attract attention on the street. There are only a few fag types who compulsively overplay their role.

If a stranger comes into the bar, the owner and the waiters make clear to him with some revealing remark or gesture what sort of bar this is.

As long as Jürgen is sober, he brusquely turns away any approaches that are made to him. If he's drunk, he makes a scene: What kind of a place is this where you get molested by men?

If he is just a bit high, he plays cat-and-mouse with the older men.

He stares straight in front of him and acts as if he hasn't noticed the hand that is on his knee and gradually creeping higher. When the hand begins to grope for his penis, he gets up and goes to the men's room.

He once gets a bit of a shock there. A man is standing with his back against the wall of the men's room with his pants down. Another man is standing up against him and thrusting his penis between the other's thighs.

Once, he follows a man of about thirty. The minute he leaves the bar, he begins to feel like a little girl.

He won't hurt me, he says to himself.

He often has this feeling when he is standing next to big, strong men. It gets more pronounced if one puts an arm around his shoulders.

·   ·   ·

Then he feels like saying: I'll do anything you like as long as you don't hurt me.

But at the same time he is speechless with fear and timidity.

Here, unlock the door, the man says, and he gives Jürgen the key. Then he gets behind Jürgen, shoves his hips against Jürgen's buttocks, and begins thrusting. He reaches around Jürgen and puts both his hands on Jürgen's penis.

Jürgen can't find the keyhole. He regrets his decision to follow the man. It wasn't even a decision. He just let himself be carried along out of curiosity.

Boy, are you twitchy, the man says. Here, give me the key. He lets go of Jürgen and opens the door.

The building is an old one built before World War I. There is an undefinable musty smell in the air. Jürgen begins to get scared when they reach the first landing. He wants to turn back. I hope the door isn't locked, he thinks.

The man grabs him by the arm, pulls him close, and kisses him hard. Jürgen slips down to the floor. The man bends down to pick him up.

Jürgen's only thought is: I've got to calm him down and get him in a good mood, got to be nice to him.

He reaches for the man's fly and opens it. The man helps him along and shoves his erect penis into Jürgen's hand. Deeper, the man groans, deeper; and he thrusts with his hips.

Jürgen senses how a woman feels who does something for the sake of maintaining domestic peace, and he starts to masturbate the man. Then he tries to get up and run away again. But the man realizes what he's up to.

He pushes Jürgen down against the steps and places his lower arm across Jürgen's throat. At the same time, he thrusts more and more rapidly into Jürgen's hand. With every movement of the man's hips, the pressure on Jürgen's throat increases. He can hardly breathe.

Stop! You're choking me, he gasps.

·　·　·

The man moans and breathes deeply. Jürgen is about to pass out. The man goes into a spasm and drops down onto Jürgen with all his weight, then pours his semen into Jürgen's hand with long, slow motions. Jürgen feels himself being choked to death.

A lot of thoughts ran through my head, he says. So this is the end. Strangled to death by a fag in a stairway. It's all over with the great philosopher.

All over with the dreams of leading a quiet life someday, of having a small business, a nice wife, and two children, of going for walks in the woods on Sunday and picking mushrooms, of whittling toy bows and arrows for the children, of going out for an evening with the wife and then home to bed for a good lay, of going to the city cemetery on a nice gray November morning to visit his parents' graves.

Jürgen sees a milky-white light before his eyes. A sharp, whining voice speaks high above him.
What's going on here?
Someone picks him up. He's unsteady on his legs. A voice near him says: My friend was feeling sick. I think I'll take him out into the fresh air.

The stairway gradually becomes more distinct to Jürgen. The scolding voice above him says: Get out of here, you scum. Jürgen turns to look.
There seems to be an old man with a huge dog on the next landing.

This is Jürgen's first and only adult homosexual adventure.

4 6 Jürgen's new friends, his experiences with Uwe, the gay bars, the hangovers that follow on his alcoholic euphoria only add to his confusion.
They all represent nothing more than excursions into a world in which he could not live. There is no escape from the life laid out for

him in N.; no escape from his family and its way of life; no escape from the social norms of the lower middle class of N., norms he cannot ignore because of his family and the business; no escape from his training, from working for customers.

What can you do? You are confronted by your life over and over again. You've got to go to church at least once a month for the sake of business. When you go to do some work in someone's house, you see how most of your fellow men live. And you join the clubs and have a drink in the bars in N. because that's where you grew up. You have to show your face every once in a while.

Adolf and Edith have very little sense of the double life Jürgen is leading. Herbert runs into him sometimes in K. He has some idea of what's going on, but he keeps it to himself. Adolf proves to be surprisingly liberal. If Jürgen turns up at the workshop in the morning looking too pathetic, Adolf sends him home to get a couple of hours more sleep. Sometimes he even sends him home at noon: Go catch up on your sleep, son.

If Jürgen makes up some excuse for quitting at noon so he can meet Uwe, Adolf doesn't object. At first there was trouble when Jürgen stayed out all night and didn't turn up until the next morning, looking the worse for wear. We're not running a hotel here where everybody can come and go as they please, Adolf growls.

Bit by bit family discipline crumbles. Whenever Adolf's refusal to grant his sons a certain freedom becomes a chronic sore point, he makes a concession. The first disagreements are over the boys' staying up in the evening. Next is their going out. Then, when they're supposed to be home. At some point, Adolf gets tired of checking up on when his sons come home at night. At some point, he no longer has the energy to make a fuss about it the next morning.

For years, Adolf struggles to maintain family life according to his views of it. One of his maxims is that the family does everything together on Sunday: breakfast, a walk in the river park while Edith cooks, noon meal, an excursion in the afternoon, coffee, and supper.

The excursions are always the same: a cruise on a river steamer, an outing to the Burgcafé in the woods, a visit to Uncle Erich's.

You can't stay in bed as long as you want even on Sundays, Jürgen used to say, while still a child. The Sunday-morning walk and the afternoon outing become problematic. Jürgen's refusal to come along is seen as a threat to the family. Herbert rarely refuses. He had more family feeling, Edith says.

When Jürgen and, later, Herbert begin to go their own ways more often, Adolf regales them with everything Edith does for them.

Your mother isn't your servant, Adolf argues. She cooks for you, cleans up your room, makes your beds, washes and mends your clothes, and worries about you, and then you march off and do as you please without a care in the world.

The boys are taken aback. They have been given to understand that it's Edith's duty to take care of her husband and children. There has never been any mention of doing anything for her in return. Herbert's response is worthy of Adolf himself: Isn't that why we have to give you money for room and board?

Against his better judgment, Jürgen offers a different argument: Then why doesn't she just quit doing all that stuff?

And who will make your bed?

Nobody.

And who will cook for you?

I won't starve.

Edith deals with the gradual collapse of family discipline by saying: The children are bound to grow up sometime. That's when you begin to realize you're getting old.

She can always come up with some appropriate words of wisdom that will relieve her of responsibility no matter what situation she finds herself in.

Adolf is most persistent in his criticism of Jürgen's clothes.

During Jürgen's genius phase, Adolf would say: Where are you off to, a ragpickers' ball? When I see you looking like that, I'm ashamed to claim you as my son.

Now he says: Do you always have to deck yourself out like that? You look like some goddam dandy. When I was young, only the pimps went around looking like that.

Pimps live off their girl friends and pick up some extra change from gambling and petty theft.

Edith kisses her son tenderly: You look just fine, Jürgen. If I were twenty years younger, I could fall in love with you myself.

4 7   Adolf and Edith have different problems with Herbert. He has a different kind of mind from Jürgen's. But because so many young men are like him he isn't an unusual case.

Like Jürgen, he goes to *Realschule*, but he does not make any effort to go to the *Gymnasium*. He reads a lot, too, but his reading is limited to adventure stories and science fiction. By the time he is fourteen, he has read seventy-two volumes of Karl May, all of Dominik, and much of Jules Verne.

From the time he is ten, he plays soccer in the Tuspo 96, first on the schoolboy team, later on the junior team. He makes the first string when he is seventeen. Year after year, his team finishes the season ranked somewhere in the middle of the A-league.

He too has his dreams. His coach wonders why he runs so strangely. Even at home, he is constantly making odd motions and freezing in peculiar poses. Adolf and Edith, who are by now somewhat accustomed to Jürgen's uncontrolled expressions of his inner life, still cannot help registering some surprise at Herbert's behavior.

·   ·   ·

Jürgen explains to his parents what Herbert is up to. His movements and poses are taken from slow-motion films of soccer players. Herbert is imitating what he sees in the TV playbacks of soccer games.

Herbert's other interest is cars. The walls of the children's room are covered with pictures of cars. He owns a whole library of books about cars. By the time he is twelve, he knows all the different makes and models and all about how cars work.

His performance in school suffers because of these outside interests. He reads into the night and falls asleep at school in the morning. He lies on his bed and arranges his file cards for hours at a time. At thirteen, he has a file of all cars readily available on the market. He enters all the soccer scores in large notebooks.

If anyone asks him if he's going to be a soccer player, he acts embarrassed. The sports magazines encourage this with their stories about famous professional soccer players who started out modestly in third-rate amateur clubs. The boys identify with their famous models.

The everyday reality of sports soon brings them back down to earth. Even the two evenings a week they have to practice if they want to stay on a team take their toll. By the time they are fourteen, most players have had their first injuries.

Herbert's passion for cars is soon directed into normal channels, too. A mechanic who works for the Opel dealer and lives on Freiligrath-strasse has a pit and a small lift in his two-car garage. He repairs cars for his friends, relatives, and neighbors, charging them for his labor by the hour. His customers have to supply the parts. The parts departments at the dealerships are set up to accommodate people who pick up parts themselves.

Every evening, every Saturday, and during his vacation, Hans Kam-prath can be found in his workshop. There are always three or four customers waiting. He has a case of beer in one corner. People help themselves and put money in a tin can. Men get together at Hans Kamprath's and talk cars. They pick his brains about what's wrong with their cars, learn tips on how to do different things, and find out where there's a good buy in a used car. Anyone who is a friend of Kamprath's can save 50 percent on repair and maintenance costs.

4 8   During his last three years in school, Herbert is at Kamprath's several times a week. Hans likes this alert youngster who knows so much about cars. He doesn't have any children himself, and Herbert could be his son. Before long, he's letting him help. After a few months, Herbert is allowed to make minor repairs and do routine maintenance work.

Adolf doesn't like it.

A boy your age should be at home in the evening. Doesn't he realize that Kamprath is exploiting him?

Adolf's attitude changes when he has to get his own crate through inspection. Kamprath gets the car in shape and takes it into the inspection station himself during his morning break.

We've never gotten a car through inspection so cheap. I wouldn't have thought they'd ever let it through again.

It's taken for granted that Herbert will train to be a mechanic when he's through school. Kamprath gets him a job where he works. On Sundays, Kamprath goes along on rallies to do tune-up work on the cars. Herbert joins him on these trips.

He is all enthused. When I've finished my apprenticeship, I'm going to drive in rallies, too. Kamprath doesn't approve. Don't get mixed up in that stuff. Rallies are great to go to. You're out in the fresh air and in the countryside, but just think how much it costs. The wear and tear on a rally car is wicked. It'll eat up every last cent you've got unless you have a rich father.

·   ·   ·

Do what I do. I go along for the ride. It gives you a chance to get out of the house and away from Mother for a while. But don't mess around with racing yourself.

When Kamprath says "Mother," he means his wife Käthe. He calls other men's wives "Mother," too. If he's in the Gasthaus zur Mitte and there happens to be a woman in the company, he'll ask the man with her, as he grandly orders a round of drinks for everyone: "And what will Mother have?"

Kamprath's "Mother" puts in an appearance only in the morning when she goes shopping and in the afternoon when she works in the yard. She's busy from morning till night. She never rests, even when she's outside in the yard. She's hard at work every minute. The house is so clean and neat that it looks as if no one lives in it. And, in fact, the Kampraths use only their kitchen and their bedroom.

The living room and dining room are hardly ever used. When the Kampraths moved into this house in the late fifties, they bought new furniture, rugs, and curtains for all the rooms. They put some of their old furniture in a large room in the cellar that was originally intended as a playroom for the children.

But there were no children. Käthe was the first to move into the cellar. What do I need a beautiful living room for if I'm just going to sit alone all the time? It's much cozier down here, and we'll save money on oil. Before long, the TV, the liqueur bottles, and the electric heater were in the cellar, too.

The Kampraths usually see each other only at breakfast at six-thirty before Hans goes to work and in the evening at supper before he disappears into his workshop. But sometimes they sit down together— when one of them has a birthday or on Sunday evenings or at Christmas.

Then Käthe says, ensconced in her cellar: We have it good here. I'm glad we decided to build our own place when we did.

And Kamprath says: No question about it. It was worth it for the garage alone.

And sometimes they even use their living room—when the Schütrumpfs come to visit, for example. Then Hans Kamprath says: I could kick myself that I didn't take my master's license back then and set up my own business.

Adolf answers: You'd be driving yourself crazy now if you had, Hans. Believe me, you're far better off. There's nothing much worse than being an independent tradesman these days. You've got a regular paycheck coming in every week, and you can earn a little extra on the side with your workshop. I couldn't dream of having a living room like this on what I make.

But it's not the money that counts for me, Adolf, Kamprath objects.

Do you think it is for me, either? Adolf asks.

Herbert knows what it is that counts. He uses his savings to buy two junked cars that were in accidents and spare parts out of some other cars that are being stripped down.

He tinkers away in Kamprath's workshop for months on end. Kamprath helps him whenever he has time. The boy's enthusiasm is infectious.

On his eighteenth birthday—and not a day later—Herbert gets his driver's license. In Pogunke's driving school, of course. The big BMW he has put together stands waiting for him in front of his house.

4 9 That all happens in January, 1971. Adolf Schütrumpf has less than four more years to live, and Jürgen has taken his first vacation trip the preceding summer. His apprenticeship is a good two years behind him. Herbert is in the second year of his. He pays for his expensive car from what he earns working at Kamprath's in his spare time. When the car becomes too expensive for him to keep, he sells it and makes a handy little profit on it.

Adolf has had some supplementary income for quite a while now, too. Edith's brother Bübi has gone a lot further in this world than his brother-in-law Adolf Schütrumpf. He began medical school the same year that Adolf started his business, married Edith, and saw his first son born.

In the 1960s, Bübi assumes a full professorship at the University of M. and starts buying land. Academics snap up tracts on the outskirts of the major university towns. The medical-school faculties are most heavily represented in this class of new landowners. Their lust for real estate is insatiable.

Toward the end of the sixties, when many of this breed begin putting their money into bombed-out buildings in West Berlin as a tax dodge, Bübi recalls that he still has a sister and a brother-in-law in his hometown of K. Bübi disowned his brother Bobo when Bobo married that hairdresser.

Bübi gradually buys up four old apartment houses built before World War I. They are dilapidated wrecks of buildings, places where only the socially down-and-out will live—old people on inadequate pensions, alcoholics, students, foreign workers, people who have no way to defend themselves.

Adolf agrees to look after these buildings. A tradesman is ideal for the job. He knows how to deal with other tradesmen and get repairs done at minimum cost.
   One thing about the lower middle class that Bübi truly appreciates is its extreme need for self-denial.

Adolf has always been a tenant himself and has constantly been at war with his landlord over things like raises in rent, repairs the landlord is responsible for, a better kitchen stove, the installation of gas heat to replace the dirt-producing coal stoves. Out of habit and miserliness, Adolf insists on using soft coal in them. The heating has been a major sore point in the family for years.

Edith complains about the filth, the ashes, the buckets of coal she has to carry up from the cellar every day. The apartment is freezing in the morning; the stoves keep going out all the time. Adolf refuses to put in gas heat at his own expense. That's the landlord's job, and if he puts in gas heat, he'll charge more rent.

As a tenant, Adolf goes wild if the landlord's agent informs him that a neighbor has lodged a complaint against him: His sons walked on the neighbor's lawn, or his dog pissed on somebody else's door. He'd bothered the neighbors by sawing and pounding nails in his kitchen after 10 p.m. The front door wasn't locked at night and the hall light had been left on.

Now that he is representing a landlord himself, he does unto his tenants as his landlord has done unto him. When they request anything of him, he forgets that he has made similar requests himself. He is a despot who squeezes out every last penny. Adolf is the scourge of the buildings he runs for his brother-in-law Bübi. Nothing is put back into them, nothing is repaired. Adolf passes on the rent money to Bübi without deducting any significant amount for operating expenses. He keeps a hundred marks per building per month for himself. Five percent of total rent received.

5 0   It is 1973. Christmas is just around the corner. Christmas is a focal point in the emotional life of the Schütrumpf family. As long as the children are young, the emphasis is on presents. Weeks before Christmas, Adolf starts dropping hints about the presents to come.

For almost a month ahead, Christmas is used as a tool to control the children's behavior: If you're a good boy, then . . .
  Violations of family discipline draw the threat: Well, then, you won't get anything for Christmas.

During December, feeling rises to a crescendo. The Advent Sundays, the Advent wreath with its candles, the cookies, Santa Claus, and the Christmas market are all stations on the way to the apotheosis of Christmas itself.

Once the Christmas goose and the tree have been bought, the symbols of the event are present in the house in concrete form.

Tension rises to a peak on the night before Christmas Eve and explodes on the twenty-fourth itself. The children's frantic excitement has reached an intolerable level. Edith is irritable; Adolf's hectic preparations give rise to fits of anger.

By noon, the family celebration is teetering on the edge of disaster. Since early morning, Adolf has been making salads, baking cakes, preparing the goose, issuing orders. Edith's role has been reduced to that of kitchen girl. Everything she does is wrong.

A thousand things are still missing for the cooking, the baking, the holidays ahead. The children have to keep running to the store and handing Adolf whatever he needs. Their ability to concentrate is near zero. All their attention is focused on the gifts to come.

Adolf feels under pressure. The children want to help decorate the tree this year, but Adolf reserves that too as his privilege. At Christmas, Father puts on a special party for his family. If anything is missing now, if anything breaks or goes wrong, the atmosphere becomes explosive. All it takes is a word of criticism from Edith: What are you so nervous about?

That does it.

Okay, the show is all yours. Doors slam; first the apartment door, then the door to the building. The car starts with a roar.

One of the as yet unexplained mysteries of the male psyche is the soothing influence a bar exerts on it. With the help of a few beers and double shots, Adolf can conquer problems that clergymen, sociologists, political scientists, and economists will never solve as long as they live.

. . .

When he comes back relaxed and cheerful two or three hours later, Edith has finished in the kitchen and the children have decorated the tree. Händel's *Largo* is on the record player. The boys are still as keyed up as ever. Adolf apologizes, has a cup of coffee and a piece of stollen, adds the finishing touches to the herring salad and the potato salad, gets the special Crakow sausages from the pantry, and tells Edith to get supper ready.

The first thing the Schütrumpfs do on Christmas Eve is eat potato salad and steamed Cracow sausages. Then comes the magic moment.

Adolf locks his wife and sons in the children's room and starts rummaging around in the bedroom. Then they can hear him arranging things in the living room. Finally, a small bell rings. Adolf is standing next to the Christmas tree, ready to greet his family fondly.

Christmas Eve is the time when Adolf's paternal generosity reaches a high point. Everything comes from him. Adolf slowly leads Edith and the boys to their places and expounds on the value of each present. Father has been impartial. No one has received more or less than anyone else.

He never buys anything for himself. He graciously accepts the gifts that Edith and the children have made for him, but he always adds: You really don't have to give me anything. I'm happy if I can give you all something.

Twenty-four years pass. The Christmas celebration is like a liturgy that is never changed for decades on end. The only things that change are the gifts and the goose.

In the sixties, it got harder and harder to buy a fresh goose. Since the Schütrumpfs have a freezer, they buy a frozen goose.

There wasn't much on them, Jürgen says. There was more stuffing than meat.

Edith manages to look on the bright side of this, too. Well, as far as I'm concerned the stuffing is the best part of roast goose anyhow.

As the boys get older, the only things they get for Christmas are clothes: pajamas, shirts, scarves, gloves, underwear. Edith gets mainly clothes, too. There's a set of underwear for her every year. Major articles of clothing are tried on before Christmas in the store: suits, coats, and shoes for the boys; a suit and coat for Edith. Adolf reminds them of these items on Christmas Eve. And don't forget the new slacks either, he says.

5 1 The Christmas of 1973 looks as if it will be a Christmas like any other. As a little extra for Edith this year, Adolf has a gold bracelet tucked away in his drawer. Jürgen's main gift is a Norwegian sweater. Herbert is getting two sheepskins for the front seat of his car. The goose is in the freezer; the tree is in the garden shed. For days, Adolf has been stocking the pantry with food and drink.

Adolf has been a heavy drinker for years. He drinks three to four bottles of beer every evening, as well as two bottles of schnapps every week. That comes to about eight or ten shots each night. Edith knows. She orders the beer. Adolf has a habit of putting empty schnapps bottles behind the sofa.

At Christmas there's red wine, French cognac, and champagne as well. Later in the evening, Adolf goes back to his old standbys. Now that's what I call a real drink after all that fancy stuff.

Adolf undermines his health with other things besides alcohol. He loves fatty foods. For breakfast he eats liverwurst and cracklings. Two of his favorite dishes are pig's feet and pork ribs with sauerkraut. Bread and drippings is a treat. The Schütrumpfs' diet is generally poor in vitamins. They eat very little fruit, very few fresh vegetables. Their mainstays are carbohydrates and ready-made soups and gravies.

Adolf's eating habits have taken their toll on him. His belly is bloated. He is considerably overweight. His walk and his movements are ponderous. He has edema in his legs that sometimes rises up to his stomach. His heart is pathologically enlarged. He has arteriosclerosis, which affects both his speech and his thought processes. Sometimes he tells the same story three times in one evening. The stories from his youth and the early days of his marriage are reduced now to a few stereotypical sentences.

Edith tries in vain to talk him into healthier habits. You should get more exercise, go for a walk more often, go swimming.

Adolf uses the car to go even the shortest distances. His Sunday-morning walk has not gone beyond the Gasthaus zur Mitte for years. The afternoon outing always ends in a bar or restaurant.

If Edith forgets to order beer or suggests cutting back on food, he claims she begrudges him his little pleasures. You don't need to be stingy, he says. I'll leave you well enough off. I'd rather die ten years earlier than do without beer and wurst.

On December 22, a neighbor watches him get out of his car. He is staggering and having difficulty standing up at all. He leaves the car door open. He holds himself up by hanging on to the fence. The neighbor thinks he's drunk. She goes up to the Schütrumpfs' later to tell them that the car door is still open.

Edith helps him undress and go to bed. It's nothing, he says. Just this blasted leg.

Adolf hates the idea of being sick. He likes to boast about his excellent health. He claims he'll live to eighty-six, just like his paternal grandfather.

The leg provides him with a good excuse. An injury suffered in an accident is no disease. Adolf had an accident two years ago. He does a lot of moonlighting on Saturdays. The money he takes in during the week goes on the books and is subject to taxes. What he makes on Saturdays he doesn't have to share with anybody.

On Saturdays, Adolf is his own man. He hangs a roof gutter here, puts in a drain there, installs soil pipes in a house that an official in the bureau of taxation is having built by moonlighters.

This kind of thing is done a lot nowadays. Many individuals who want to build a house can't afford the prices that building contractors are charging. In N. and in the villages around K., every other new house is built by moonlighters who claim they're just helping a neighbor out.

This arrangement is hard on both the owner and the men doing the work. A lot of men in construction trades work every evening of the week and every weekend on top of their regular jobs. Some owners wreck themselves physically working on their new houses. Some even damage their health permanently and retire at forty.

Adolf's accident happens on a Saturday.

He has not taken adequate safety precautions, as always when the cost of safety on the job can't be charged to the customer. He is installing chimney flashing, starts to slip, manages to catch hold of the roof gutter. If he'd been younger, he might have been able to pull himself up again, but he can't do it and falls into a flower bed. He's had a bad knee ever since.

From that time on, Adolf has blamed everything on his bum leg.

5 2   By evening, Adolf is only half conscious. He is delirious, tells Edith how to stuff the goose, asks if there is enough beer in the house.

Edith calls the doctor. He isn't surprised. Adolf had been to see him two days before. The doctor had figured something like this would happen. Adolf has kept Edith completely in the dark. When the ambulance arrives, Adolf is unconscious. Herbert is away on a skiing vacation. Jürgen is out and can't be located.

At four o'clock the next afternoon, Jürgen is at Adolf's bedside. Edith was at the hospital in the morning. Hepatic coma, the doctor in charge says.

It's me, Father, he says softly. What are you doing in here?

Adolf is restless. He tosses around in his bed. His body is soaked with sweat. All he has on is a short undershirt. His lower body is naked. Jürgen pulls the light covers over his bloated body. He kicks them off again right away.

Out, he says, out. And he tries to get up. Jürgen pushes him back down. Stay in bed. You've got to rest.

Adolf can't be reasoned with. He signals to Jürgen. Jürgen bends down over him. Adolf says: Out, out. He throws his arms around Jürgen's shoulders and wants him to help him get up.

Several times he signals that Jürgen should check to see if his wallet is still in the drawer of the bedside table.

When Jürgen leaves, his father mumbles that he should bring him something the next time he comes, a good healthy chunk of wurst. Jürgen isn't sure that his father has even recognized him.

After two weeks, Adolf's mind is relatively clear again for the first time. Hanging on to Jürgen's arm, he walks a few steps in his room. The doctor's responses to Jürgen's questions are vague. Jürgen describes to him how Adolf looked before this attack. He was an incredibly energetic, well-nourished man.

Now his cheeks are sunken. The bones of his skull stand out prominently. There are dark brown spots on his legs. His voice is almost inaudible. He is hardly able to express himself, and his movements are severely limited.

The doctor continues to be evasive. He can't say what's wrong with Adolf or how serious his illness is. He's not prepared to say what he thinks Adolf's chances for survival are either.

Adolf is discharged after six weeks.

By the spring of 1974, it is obvious that he cannot work anymore. He soils himself often and can do hardly anything for himself. He walks with a shuffling gait. It's difficult for him to think or speak clearly. He often sits for hours at a time as if in a trance. Sometimes he's himself again for a half hour; then his mind begins to wander.

You've got to concentrate on staying alive. You've got to toe the line and follow the doctor's orders, Jürgen says.

Adolf nods meekly.

All right, Jürgen. If you say so.

He drinks diet beer and follows the other rules laid down for him.

5 3   The business suffers. At Easter, the Schütrumpfs let Käse go. They have work aplenty, but Jürgen just can't seem to manage things. He doesn't know how to make estimates, figure materials, write bills. He has trouble buying supplies and dealing with customers. He can't set up a smooth work schedule.

A few times, Jürgen takes Adolf along with him to see customers. Adolf talks with them reasonably, listens to what they have to say, makes suggestions. Suddenly he seems to step into another existence. He tells them where they should put the stairway in, explains how to clean a chimney and reline a stove. He warns them to avoid poisonous mushrooms and tells them how to recognize them. Later on, he gives advice on working the black market.

Jürgen breaks off the visit and takes Adolf home. I'll call back tomorrow, he says.

Adolf turned fifty-nine in the fall. He looks eighty.

Edith and Herbert seem to accept Adolf's rapid aging as if it were normal. Jürgen is like a hunter watching his prey. The similarity between infancy and senility, the apparent regression to an infantile state, makes it impossible for Jürgen to be of any real help. Mesmerized, he sits and stares at his father, taking note of his difficulties and incapacities.

Several times he tries to draw his father into conversation. Now that you're so sick and almost died, do you sometimes think about the meaning of life? Are you left with anything? Has it been worthwhile to live?

Adolf stares at him. It looks as though he is beginning to grasp the question. He smiles as if he were remembering something. Then he sinks back in his chair.

Oh, Jürgen, there's a lot I could tell you.

Then tell me.

What for?

Jürgen is the first to mention the possibility of selling the business. We'll have to close the business down before we owe more than our stuff is worth. I can look for a job.

Adolf resists. Give up the business? He says he'll be on his feet again before long.

He also resists selling the car. It's still standing where Adolf left it months ago. The registration and insurance are a continuing and needless expense.

Another insurance premium is due next month.

Are you trying to tell me I'm running out of money? Adolf asks.

Edith sells the car on the sly. Adolf is too weak to get upset. All he says is: If I don't have the car anymore, I might as well lie down and die right now.

He has Jürgen count out the money Edith got for the car. Then he sends Jürgen to the bank with it and insists on seeing the deposit slip when he comes back.

On Good Friday, Uncle Hans Mehlig and his wife, Anni, come to visit. The women sit in the kitchen while the men struggle to keep a conversation going in the living room.

Edith describes Adolf's illness in great detail and complains about how much work it is to take care of him. He no longer has full control over his bladder or his bowels.

His underwear has to be changed daily. He has to spend most of his time lying down. Sometimes Edith has to change the sheets every day, too. It's hard for him to wash himself. Edith tells how difficult it is to wash such a heavy, helpless man every day and keep him clean. She airs the bedroom out all the time, but it still smells as if something were rotting in there.

Jürgen sees the Mehligs downstairs to the front door. He asks if he could have a job at Fahlbusch & Siebert. Uncle Hans says yes without hesitating.

Things aren't too rosy in our business right now, but for the son of an old friend. . . . After all, I've known you since you were knee high to a grasshopper.

It's because of Father, Jürgen says. His parents can't live on what he and Herbert pay for their room and board.

Who knows if Father will get any kind of pension or not, Jürgen adds.

They'll have to give him something, Mehlig says.

But when? says Jürgen.

That night at supper he says: I'll start work at Uncle Hans's firm next Tuesday.

I can't stop you, Adolf says. I've got to lie down.

He looks sad. I've gone and slaved for twenty-five years just so my son can throw the whole thing over.

5 4   The history of N. is closely linked to the history of Fahlbusch & Siebert. The position the plant occupies now is a direct result of the economic policies the elector adopted in the nineteenth century. The ruling house and the landed aristocracy opposed the industrialization of the state.

Don't talk to me about free enterprise, the elector used to say. If we have that, we'll bring down the greatest plague of the century on our heads—the proletariat. If once you have free enterprise, the next thing you'll have is workers' coalitions and a lot of trouble on your hands.

The ambiguous situation that middle-class merchants and manufacturers came to occupy in K. was the inevitable result of the elector's policy.

People like Fahlbusch differ from the middle-class administrators, the court aristocracy, and the major landowners, who are almost all aristocrats, too, by creating new technologies with their major and minor inventions and increasing both productive capacity and output of goods. Thus, it is their economic activity that improves the standard of living for the lower classes and helps lessen the shocking extremes of social inequality. In this sense, the difference is a positive one.

But on the other hand, the Fahlbusches adhere strictly to the given constitutional framework and never question the established legal system. They are interested in acquiring privileges, not power. Their behavior in the revolutions of 1830, 1848, and 1918 demonstrates this.

The state is a nuisance to them if it interferes with the pursuit of their economic goals. But it is a welcome ally if it maintains the law and order that promote their work and if it wages wars from which industry can profit.

Under the elector's economic policy, the lower classes live idle lives that profit no one. What is new about the Fahlbusches and others like them is their method for exploiting these classes even more through work. Only reluctantly—and in exchange for a sizable sum—does the elector grant the blacksmith Gottlieb Fahlbusch permission to build a factory in N. in 1836.

N. lies barely three kilometers from the outskirts of the city. It is a relatively well-to-do village where only some of the inhabitants still make a living from farming.

The commercial possibilities are favorable. The road to Frankfurt passes through N. It is one of the three major arteries leading out of K. The other two connect K. with Leipzig and with the Netherlands.

The Fahlbusches have profited from N.'s location for generations.

They run the post office, an inn, a smithy, and a large farm. In the boom years following the founding of the Second Reich in 1871, when K. expands rapidly in the direction of N. and swallows up the smaller town, a Fahlbusch makes respectable profits by selling his farm holdings as building sites.

In the 1820s, Gottlieb Fahlbusch, working in his father Johann's smithy, begins manufacturing cabinets that are lined with metal and that serve as iceboxes. Twice a week, horse-drawn wagons drive through the streets of K. selling blocks of ice that have been cut from ponds and flooded meadows during the winter and stored in deep cellars.

In 1836, the Fahlbusches move their icebox production out of the smithy.

They put up their first factory buildings on one of their fields located along Frankfurter Strasse and closer to the city. These first two structures are small decorative brick buildings that look like chapels. They have battlements and pinnacles, a rose window on the gable over the entranceway facing Französische Strasse, and buttresses designed to look like the columns of a Greek temple.

Gottlieb Fahlbusch goes to the *Gymnasium* in K. and studies at the academy of art. He gets his practical training in his father's workshop during his spare time. He studies architecture and designs the first buildings of the new factory himself. One of the buildings houses the production area. Fahlbusch has his offices and his apartment in the other.

In 1843, Fahlbusch is granted a concession to establish a foundry, and he starts casting stove parts. Some of the stove plates he produces are enameled in different colors and decorated with ornamental patterns and figures that recur over and over again. These plates are then assembled into three chambers, one on top of another, and the completed stove can weigh as much as four hundred pounds. The smoke passes through a baffle system formed by the chambers and heats the iron plates. In the past, almost every house had one of these stoves. After World War II, people got rid of them as scrap metal.

Having started out producing stoves and iceboxes, the firm stays in these areas and becomes known in the later decades of its history as a manufacturer of heating and refrigeration systems. Only after 1945 does Siebert develop a third line of specialization, air conditioning.

5 5   For N., this new firm is a great boon. In the nineteenth century, farmers' sons all over the country migrate into the cities and industrial centers to find work. From the southern part of the electorate they go as far as the Ruhr and the area around Siegen.

Many emigrate to North America. Others serve in the elector's army, which is much too large, considering the economic resources and the strategic needs of the small state.

With the help of this army, the elector tries to hold his own in the power struggle between Bavaria to the south, Hanover and England to the north, and Prussia to the east. His efforts are in vain, as the events of 1866 show.

The agrarian structure in the principality of H. is such that only one son can stay on a farm. The farms are too small to support more than one family. This surplus of manpower insures the existence of a reserve army to implement military policy.

The people from the countryside around K. go to work in the new factories. The material circumstances of the village populations gradually improve, and a new class develops: small-scale farmers who work in the factories and do their farm work on the side.

This is what happens in N., too. But, unlike men and women elsewhere who have to get up at four or five to get to work, the farmers in N. have their workplace practically in their front yard.

Even in the nineteenth century, the Fahlbuschers form a special class in N. and the surrounding area. Working for Fahlbusch is a privilege that raises a worker above the other members of his class. A Fahlbuscher is like a civil servant. He joins the company as an apprentice and stays there until retirement. Gottlieb Fahlbusch, who runs the company until his death at the age of eighty-four in 1888, encourages this tendency.

When Prussia annexes the electorate in 1866, the firm has eighty employees. N. has barely a hundred households. A man from almost every family works for Fahlbusch. In some families, it's two or three.

Fahlbusch establishes the first canteen in K. and environs, also the first company health plan and the first company housing development. The men's glee club from Fahlbusch & Son has thirty members. Working-class songs are never sung. In the winter, the Fahlbuschers receive part of their wages in the form of coupons for winter potatoes and coal. As late as the 1890s, the potatoes still come from Fahlbusch's fields.

In 1888, when Gottlieb dies, Fahlbusch has two hundred employees. They felt that Gottlieb was one of them. He stood at the factory gate in the morning before work began and didn't go through the gate and into his office himself until all the rest of his flock had arrived. Johann Gottlieb Fahlbusch, the oldest grandson of the firm's founder, takes over. Johann Gottlieb's father, Christian, dies of leukemia a few months after Gottlieb's death.

The firm's style changes under Johann Gottlieb's leadership. The hierarchical structure of the company becomes more obvious. The plant is a mirror image of a society in which everyone has his assigned place. The company housing, which Johann Gottlieb expands considerably, reveals this structure to even the casual observer.

The row houses for the workers that were built after 1871 stand along Frankfurter Strasse between Französische Strasse and Industriestrasse. They are basically two-story buildings but have attic apartments as well. The apartments are small, consisting of only a combination kitchen and sitting room, two bedrooms, and a storeroom.

They have no bathrooms. At first there is no running water. The toilets and the water faucets are in the courtyards.

Each apartment has a small yard for a garden and a stonework stall for the pigs, rabbits, and chickens.

The houses for the foremen, the technicians, and the office staff are freestanding three-family houses with balconies and porches. Each apartment has a living room, two bedrooms, kitchen, bath, entrance hall, pantry, and workroom. These buildings are equipped with central heating installed by Fahlbusch, of course. Lawn makes up at least part of the yard, and no provision is made for keeping animals.

The houses for the company's top officials have large yards and are separated from the rest of the housing development by a major street. They also have a coach house and a small cottage for the couple who look after the house and grounds.

The crowning glory of the development is the Fahlbusch family's villa, which was built in 1895. The house is surrounded by a private park with large shade trees in it. An elaborate wrought-iron fence runs around the park. The arrangement reminds Jürgen of Richard Wagner's villa, Wahnfried, in Bayreuth. The villa and park are located on Französiche Strasse next to the original factory buildings Gottlieb Fahlbusch built.

The grounds the plant occupies triple in size between 1836 and 1888. At the turn of the century, they will double once more. The buildings put up in 1836 represent only about one tenth of the present complex.

In 1926, the engineer Dr. Erich Siebert marries Johann Gottlieb's only daughter. Johann Gottlieb dies at the age of seventy-nine in 1939. The reconstruction of the firm after 1945 falls to Siebert, who renames it Fahlbusch & Siebert. He dies in 1960. He has no children. His widow, Wilhelmine, born in 1901, is his sole heir.

Uncle Hans Mehlig is one of three directors in this firm.

5 6 When Jürgen Schütrumpf starts working for Fahlbusch & Siebert on the Tuesday after Easter in 1974, the firm still has an excellent reputation, but its image of old is not entirely untarnished. Only some of the six hundred employees still consider it a special honor to be a Fahlbuscher. They are mostly older men.

Very few employees feel they have any kind of relationship at all with the owner. Old Siebert upheld tradition by making a daily tour of the plant, talking with his workers, and interviewing prospective employees.

His widow never sets foot in the factory. The younger employees know of her only by hearsay and through occasional articles and pictures in the local press. She is shown standing with the widows of deceased company employees, presenting a gift to an employee who has been with the firm for thirty or forty or fifty years, or unveiling a memorial plaque to her great-grandfather, Gottlieb Fahlbusch, at a municipal trade school.

Jürgen's foreman is Heinrich Bachmeier. The other workers call him Bach Hein. Bach Hein is sixty years old, a giant of a man, and a dyed-in-the-wool Fahlbuscher. He is the first foreman back working for Siebert after the war. He began his apprenticeship with Fahlbusch in 1924 and got his master's license in 1935. He spent the war years on the home front because of a heart defect. He did not belong to the Nazi Party, but he is supposedly one of the witnesses who saw Mehlig beat up the foreign worker. During Mehlig's denazification in 1949, Bach Hein testifies in Mehlig's favor. He confirms that Mehlig was among those veteran Fahlbuschers who came to work in SA uniforms during the Nazi period. He assumes that Mehlig was a party member as well. He has nothing but praise for Mehlig's behavior at work.

The Americans appoint Bachmeier to the workers' council. The Communists in the council and some of the Social Democrats oppose and defeat him on the issue of rehiring Mehlig. This is why Mehlig cannot be officially rehired until sometime in the early fifties.

Bachmeier's name is linked with Mehlig's once again when Mehlig files his libel suit. The accused journalist says Bachmeier reportedly witnessed the beating of the foreign worker. Bachmeier denies it, but this testimony is not taken under oath. At the time, Mehlig is already head of personnel at Fahlbusch & Siebert. In the mid-sixties, he is appointed director.

Heinrich Bachmeier belongs to a generation of workers that hardly exists anymore today. He remembers the political strife before 1933 with horror.

Workers were fighting among themselves. Was that necessary? Jürgen doesn't know.

Bach looks out for Jürgen because Mehlig is personally responsible for getting him hired.

I didn't like it either when the Nazis got everybody fired who was in the KPD* or the SPD.†

I don't care whether a man was a Nazi or a Socialist.

Bach Hein judges people by other criteria: respect for the law, civil behavior, quietness, neatness, diligence, and competence.

I don't want any troublemakers around.

His loyalty to the firm is absolute. In 1955, he sees to it that the last remaining Communist is thrown out of the workers' council. The man's name is Ballschneider. On November 23 and 24, 1953, the local press reports that the workers' council has decided to petition the labor court to remove Ballschneider from the council.

The petition is granted. The court finds that Ballschneider used his office to advance the cause of the Communist Party and thereby violated section 51 of the labor law.

On several occasions, Ballschneider supposedly furnished a journalist

*Kommunistische Partei Deutschlands—TRANS.
†Sozialdemokratische Partei Deutschlands—TRANS.

from the *Sozialistische Volkszeitung* with reports of what had gone on in closed meetings of the council. This activity proved detrimental to the business interests of the firm.

In one instance, the firm was negotiating a large sale of refrigeration equipment to a foreign concern. The workers' council voted to accept management's policy of freezing wages for the coming months. This would keep the price of the equipment down and prevent the order from going to a firm whose labor costs were lower.

Ballschneider was also accused of distributing the Communist Party publication *Der Hammer*, Communist leaflets, and the *Sozialistische Volkszeitung* in the plant.

Several members of the workers' council had refused to attend meetings if Ballschneider continued to belong to it.

The firm's management was unwilling to give the council confidential information if the information was going to be published a few days later in the *SVZ*.

Mehlig, the personnel manager, is the moving force behind the proceedings against Ballschneider. Bach Hein is nothing more than his stooge. Bach Hein fails to see the parallel between the present actions of the workers' council and the measures the Nazis took against Communists in 1933.

Ballschneider considers bringing suit against other members of the workers' council. The ones who belong to the SPD and the CDU have stacks of party literature in their desks, too. The labor law forbids party propagandizing of any kind on the plant grounds.

Ballschneider decides not to take action, going on the principle that workers should not be pitted against workers.

5 7   Bachmeier's loyalty to the company goes back to the first years after the war. He helps the firm get back on its feet again. The plant had not taken any direct hits in the bombing raids. N. is a

suburb that was never a bombing target. But the plant did suffer some damage from air-delivered naval mines that missed the river and landed in the meadows along it. The roofs and windows are almost all destroyed. Some of the machinery is in need of repair.

Sixty percent of the work force at the end of the war is made up of foreign workers and POWs. About a month after the American troops move into K., some fifty of Siebert's old employees report in.

The first few weeks are spent in cleaning up the plant and making repairs.

Siebert and the firm's three directors are in an American detention camp near Darmstadt. An administrator is appointed to run Siebert's farm, but Siebert still has a large say in what is done. On one occasion, he has two hundred geese slaughtered as a treat for his friends and himself in Darmstadt.

When a certain Director Weissbrod celebrates his twenty-fifth year with the firm, the workers send a message of congratulation to him in Darmstadt. Copies of the message are posted in the plant. The text concludes with the sentence: We hope to have you back in our ranks again soon.

Theoretically, production is under the supervision of the Allied Control Council. But in reality it is the workers and the workers' council that get the plant back in running condition and supervise production. They treat anything that has come through the war unscathed as if it were their personal property. When the Allies tag some of the machinery for removal from the plant, the workers hide these machines behind a wall that they quickly build overnight and let the Allies take away some old, worthless machinery.

Bach Hein and others comb the bombed-out streets of K. with carts and horse-drawn wagons, searching for replacement parts, machines, tools, building materials, and so on. When Siebert returns from detention camp, he finds a proud work force that is fully conscious of what it can do.

.   .   .

That gives rise to problems. The party platforms and the state constitution all contain Socialistic tendencies and call for a parity of workers and management. The Communists and some Social Democrats are particularly vocal in their demand that labor have a larger say in management decisions. They postulate the equality of capital and labor.

Siebert deliberately sets about recruiting trustworthy individuals in the plant hierarchy to oppose such tendencies. In the speech he gives on his return, he thanks all the members of the work force, but he singles out some for special praise, among them Bach Hein.

And as production returns to normal and other foremen are hired, Bach Hein remains Siebert's right-hand man. When Siebert puts on his annual banquet for his political and business associates, his directors, and other high-ranking company officials, Herr and Frau Bachmeier are always invited. And every year until his death, Bachmeier gets a Christmas basket with a bottle of French cognac in it.

5 8   Bachmeier's unblemished record in political matters makes him a desirable candidate for local political office. Running on the Social Democrats' ticket in the first municipal elections held after the war, he wins a seat on the city council. Shortly after, he joins the SPD.

Early in the fifties, when a large percentage of the party is already made up of former fellow travelers of the Nazi Party, Bachmeier is a compromise figure acceptable to both the Right and the Left, and he is elected chairman of the local SPD committee.

That is not the only office he has in N. The positions he holds make him a well-known and universally respected citizen. At his funeral in 1976, representatives of the following organizations speak: local SPD committee, local union chapter, sports club Tuspo 96, Rabbit Breeders' Association, Concordia Glee Club, Lutheran church, town advisory council, marching band, fishermen's club, workers' council and management of Fahlbusch & Siebert.

A man like Bach Hein is a mainstay in the social life of a suburb like N. where everyone knows almost everyone else.

Bach Hein's relationship with Director Mehlig is not altogether happy. I don't like to be blackmailed, Herr Bachmeier, Mehlig says whenever he has to negotiate with the workers' council.

Bach Hein thinks he knows what Mehlig means. He never does anything that could be interpreted as blackmail. If he did, Mehlig might think Bach Hein was using what he knew to put pressure on him.

In the last years of his life, Bach Hein develops some enemies even in his own party, particularly among the younger members.

On a hill above N. there is a clearing in the woods. The members of the local historical society claim that this clearing is an old Germanic meeting ground. The trees that form a circle here can't be much more than a hundred and fifty years old. On December 21, some citizens of N. celebrate the winter solstice in this clearing.

The white-collar types who belong to the mountaineering and hiking club carry torches. The glee club sings a melancholy song. Later on, a bonfire is lit.

Bach Hein and the president of the local historical society give brief speeches. According to some who were present, the speakers invoked the German soil, the farmer, the Germanic spirit, and the traditions of a direct democracy in which there were still true tribal leaders, loyal followers, and no foreigners.

After the ceremony, the celebration is continued in the Gasthaus zur Mitte. The first round is on the house. Old Penzing is all fired up, recalling the days of his youth.

To the amazement of the regular clientele, Penzing sells the solstice celebrators several bottles of schnapps at cost.

·　·　·

Some guests claim that Nazi songs were sung late in the evening. The organizers of the event take exception to this. The songs were youth-movement songs from the twenties, scouting songs, military marches, songs like "With our ships full laden with the treasures of the Orient" and "Not even the seas can keep lovers apart."

When these attacks refuse to die down, Bachmeier loses patience. Didn't the Young Socialists of N. sing Red songs at their last celebration? he wants to know; songs like "March on and don't forget: solidarity!"

Wasn't it class conflict that brought disaster down on Germany in the past? Before 1933?

5 9   Jürgen's discomfort in his new job has nothing to do with politics. His reaction takes a biological rather than a political form.

He's hardly out of the house before his bowels begin to rumble. As he walks to the trolley stop, the pressure on his sphincter muscles mounts. On the ride to work, his insides calm down. Since the summer of 1972, he has owned a secondhand Opel Rekord in good condition. But he uses public transportation to go to work.

When he gets off the trolley, the pressure returns and is worse than before. He hurries to the plant gate with his buttocks squeezed together and sweat running down his face. He has regularly recurring cramps in his lower abdomen, as if he were having labor pains.

He races against time to get to the locker room. He covers the last few meters to the toilet walking just from the knees down. Stiff-legged, he makes his way into the stall. His bowels spurt out their contents with a violent splash. He is irritated to see a brown spot in his underwear.

Sometimes the urge to defecate is preceded by nausea. When he is brushing his teeth in the morning, he feels a cough coming up from his stomach. The smell of the toothpaste makes him gag; his stomach heaves. He spits up something from his stomach. Often the food from last night's supper is not fully digested.

Once he has had his coffee and is out on the street, he feels the tickling in his throat and stomach again. His coffee rises up into his mouth. He leans over the curb. His eyes fill with tears; the effort brings the blood to his head. Sometimes capillaries in his eyes break. The convulsive vomiting puts pressure on his bladder and increases the strain on his sphincter.

The smell and crowding in the locker room nauseate him, too. Sometimes he runs out the door half dressed and buttons up outside.

He is irritated by the sight of the man next to him who has just taken off his pants and is hanging them in his locker. His long baggy underwear pants slide down over his belly.

When will they just fall off him and leave his privates exposed?

The man bunches his underwear up into a thick roll to make it stay up better. Jürgen stares at this roll, stares at the huge, empty pouch that the baggy underwear forms between the man's thighs, stares at the wool socks that slide down around his ankles.

This same kind of thing happens during work. Jürgen is distracted whenever he sees another worker's underwear through the long slit in the side of his overalls. He keeps staring until somebody yells at him: Hey, you! Are you falling asleep on your feet?

He is compelled to watch when someone bends down to lift something heavy and his pants slide down in back, exposing the crack between his buttocks.

Intimacy has to be avoided at all costs. Feelings for another's body have to be suppressed. Where shared heavy work could heighten the physical sense of needing each other, of being there for each other, the body is taboo.

Men have been taught to feel their bodies only in connection with sex. They become machines in their work. Since physical contact can only mean sex, they are careful not to touch each other.

Freddy stands in front of Jürgen, out of breath.

Light me a cigarette, he says, holding out his dirty hands. I don't have any, Jürgen says.

In my left pocket.

Jürgen hesitates. What are you waiting for? Freddy asks.

With infinite caution, Jürgen feels around in Freddy's pocket, trying desperately not to touch his thigh or anything more untouchable yet. Dig down, Freddy says. I won't bite.

Jürgen can feel his heart pounding. He comes across objects in Freddy's pocket that don't feel like anything he can recognize. Somebody else's pants pocket is more terrifying than a dark lonely road through a deep forest. Jürgen's fingers strike on something hard. He wonders if it is a pocketknife.

Come on, hurry up, says Konrad. How much longer are you going to make us wait? The old man is giving us the eye already.

The old man is Bach Hein.

The hard object that Jürgen pulls out of Freddy's pocket, thinking it's his lighter, is a roll of Life Savers.

Let me, Konrad says. He stands behind Freddy, reaches his right hand into Freddy's right-hand pocket, and starts pawing around without any hesitation. Then he reaches into the left-hand pocket with his left. To do this, he has to move in close to Freddy.

Jürgen watches, fascinated but incredulous. Konrad notices his expression and starts thrusting with his hips. Freddy snaps at him: Knock it off, asshole.

Konrad takes his hands out of Freddy's pockets and says: There aren't any cigarettes in there.

Then give me one of yours.

During the morning break, Freddy pulls a leaflet out of his breast pocket. Here, read this.

6 0 Freddy's real name is Fritz Niebling. He is in his late twenties and is unmarried. He went to *Realschule* and did an apprenticeship at Fahlbusch & Siebert.

The Nieblings are Communists and anti-Fascists. Freddy's father was in a concentration camp for a while after 1933. After his release, he can't find any work in his profession as a journalist. In 1936, he gets a job in highway construction. Even though he refrains from all political activity, he is arrested several times. During the war, he is classified as unfit for service. He spends the last years of the war as a sapper.

When the war ends, he starts to work actively for the KPD. When the Communist Party is outlawed in 1956, he continues to agitate for it, distributes labor literature and leaflets, is arrested again, and sentenced to several years in prison. When he is released, he is again without work. Once the DKP* is formed, he does publicity work for it, first in K., then in W.

The only reason Freddy gets hired on as an apprentice at Fahlbusch & Siebert is the economic boom in the early sixties. Laws barring the relatives of Communists from certain jobs have not yet been introduced. The collusion between management and the government agencies responsible for surveillance of enemies of the state has not yet been developed to the extent it is now. Because of all these factors, Fritz Niebling gets a post at Fahlbusch & Siebert.

He stands out among the other apprentices because of his political awareness, his enjoyment of debate, and his energy. He is elected to represent the younger workers in the plant.

He proves to be a skillful negotiator in his dealings with the workers' council and with the plant management.

Conflicts begin to crop up only after he finishes his apprenticeship

*Deutsche Kommunistische Partei—TRANS.

and becomes a regular employee. One day, Xerox copies of the newspaper article from the fifties that dealt with Mehlig's Nazi past begin to circulate in the plant.

Next comes a leaflet criticizing the workers' council for the way it treated the Communist Ballschneider.

Another leaflet describes the close relationship that the workers' council chairman Bach Hein has with the Siebert family and accuses Bach Hein of collaborating with management against the interests of the workers.

The rumor is that Niebling wrote these leaflets or at least distributed them. Nothing can be proved. No one admits to having personally received one of these leaflets from Freddy. The workers claim that the leaflets simply turn up at different locations in the plant—in the bathrooms, in the locker rooms, in the canteen.

Mehlig files a complaint against an unknown party for disseminating the newspaper article attacking him. Since the court forced the author to retract his statements, it follows that the article has to remain out of circulation.

Freddy has been living alone in his family's three-room apartment since his father started working in W. The political police turn up at his door one day. They give Freddy the choice of letting them in or of opening himself to the charge of resisting an officer in the lawful conduct of his duties.

One of the officers says: Then we'll just say there was a likelihood of danger. For us there's always a likelihood of danger. We can get into any apartment on that one.

Later on, their conversation turns quite friendly.

The search lasts two hours. The officers take careful note of the *Complete Works of Marx and Engels* and of other classic and modern authors from the workers' movement. They also note a number of periodicals, press agency reports, and so on. Most of this literature belongs to Freddy's father.

The officers are particularly interested in Freddy's handwritten notes about Fahlbusch & Siebert. He has recorded in detail the contributions of the workers and the workers' council to the reconstruction of the firm. They confiscate these notes and a draft for a leaflet as evidence.

The leaflet claims that in view of their contributions, the workers should have been granted a voice in company policy decisions and a share in the profits.

Nothing comes of this investigation, but Freddy has been warned and is a marked man. From now on, everyone will know who the source of this kind of stuff is. For the time being, it is a good thing for him that he is not a member of the newly founded DKP or one of its subsidiary organizations.

6 1 In 1972, Freddy even goes against DKP policy.

As in many plants where the workers have only the most rudimentary political consciousness, there is a large communication gap between the workers and their elected council and representatives. The union organization is weak, and there is considerable mistrust of the council and the representatives.

The workers dutifully go through the motions of electing a workers' council and then go on grumbling among themselves.

The social structure of the work force contributes partially to this lack of morale. As early as 1853, the "Statistical Report on Economic Conditions in K." had this to say about the local industrial workers:

"Not only do they come from the peasant class and the class of rural day laborers, but some of them still belong to this class. Many of them continue to live on small pieces of land and walk to work in the factory every day. The women and children, assuming they are not working in the plant themselves, tend the fields and bring the workers a home-cooked meal at noon. In this way, the workers' families do not live exclusively from their wages but also derive a small income from their land."

As late as 1974, only a small fraction of the work force at Fahlbusch & Siebert can be called proletarian, and the major part of this group is made up of foreign workers.

The workers from the surrounding villages still have small subsistence farms. Even many of the workers living in N. own their own houses and have gardens where they grow fruit, vegetables, and potatoes. Many keep rabbits. Others buy a pig from a farmer, have it slaughtered in the village, put the meat in the freezer, and hang the sausages made from it in the attic.

Former tradesmen do moonlighting after work and on the weekends and earn a little extra that way. This helps keep alive the petty-bourgeois mentality that hampers the development of political consciousness in the work force and that prevents the workers from uniting and forcefully defending their own interests.

As a result, the opposition to the workers' council is weak and unfocused. The men under Bachmeier come to Niebling to complain and blow off steam. Niebling soon realizes that this kind of opposition is ineffective and detrimental to the solidarity of the work force.

In 1972, Freddy wants to run for a seat on the workers' council. Bach Hein values Freddy as a worker, but he opposes his candidacy, claiming Freddy is a political radical and troublemaker. The workers' council at Fahlbusch & Siebert is a closed society. Basically the same people run for it all the time.

The workers' representatives would be willing to place Freddy's name far down on the list. This in itself would not be tragic, because no one is obliged to vote for the candidates whose names appear on the top of the ballot. But in practice the workers always do check the names at the top of the list. Consequently, Freddy's chances for winning would be very slim.

Freddy and two other workers decide to present their own list. The workers' council and the personnel office do everything they can to keep this independent list out of the balloting. It is rumored about that the troublemakers may be fired. Freddy and the other two dissidents have a lot of trouble getting the signatures they need to offer an alternate list of candidates.

When the election is held, the independents get so many votes that all three of them win seats on the workers' council. The union leadership is horrified. Instead of accepting the will of the voters, it turns against the three upstarts and expels them from the union.

6 2   At Fahlbusch & Siebert, Jürgen comes face to face with two problems he has known about only by hearsay up to now: foreign workers and politics.

There are two Italians in his work area, the Pittui brothers, Francesco and Patricio.

In the world Jürgen comes from, foreign workers are considered lazy and dirty. They are fit only for simple menial work. Jürgen sees what good workers they are. At quitting time, they wash up and dress better than any of their German colleagues.

He is surprised to see that the German workers respect their foreign colleagues for what they can do and treat them pretty much as equals.

There is little personal contact among the workers. After working in the plant for several weeks, Jürgen doesn't know much more about most of his co-workers than their first names. The workers don't introduce themselves to newcomers. When they talk about themselves in the breaks, they assume that everyone knows who they are and what they're talking about. With time, a new man can form a fragmentary picture of the others from these many small details.

Freddy takes Jürgen under his wing. He is aware of Jürgen's sensitivity and excessive feelings of insecurity.

Like almost all young people born right after the war, Jürgen has had practically no political education. He has been taught to think in concepts and categories that are useless for grasping sociopolitical reality and the realities of the plant.

Political events that might have influenced him have never occurred in K. and the surrounding area. Revolutions and political changes always took place somewhere else. Nothing but a few delayed and harmless tremors has ever reached K.

The picture that people in K. got of the student movement in the sixties and seventies was the distorted one the mass media presented. There are a few institutions of higher learning in K., but any attempts at political activism remain sporadic and insignificant here among a population whose revolutionary acts, if they deserve that name at all, have always taken the form of servile petitioning of the powers that be.

Jürgen Schütrumpf is unable to grasp the concept of exploitation. The only meaning it has for him is as a polemical expression used by proponents of a political philosophy that most people reject. For decades, the state and federal politicians from K. have belonged to the Right Wing of the Social Democratic Party. As a consequence, the middle class there has strong Fascist leanings.

The language in the official job description issued by the federal bureau responsible for working conditions reveals the inhumanity of industrial organization based solely on efficiency. Jürgen's job is "Cutting Sheet Metal Strips on Plate Shears." In the column "Worker's Responsibility for Product Quality," the description says: "Avoid errors in adjustment of shears and in tending the machine."

The column "Mental Effort, Attention, Thinking" reads: "Attention required in setting shears and in placing sheet metal against stop fence."

The column "Muscular Effort" reads: "Standing all day, turning and bending when moving sheet metal from pile prior to inserting in shears. Weight per sheet: ca. 16 kg. Operation of foot switch."

The final column in the description is titled "Environmental Factors": "Discomfort due to dirty and sometimes oily sheet metal, danger of cuts from sharp metal edges despite use of leather gloves. Noise from twenty presses in the same work area. Noise level: 84 decibels A."

In this system, a man is a machine. He is considered only in terms of his function. The strains he is exposed to in his work are treated as nothing more than factors that might impair his work performance. He no longer exists as a human being who experiences his activity or suffers from it and who is deformed by the conditions he is subjected to in his work.

Jürgen spends his days confined to a small area between the sheet metal pile and the plate shears. The shop he works in measures about 10 by 35 meters and contains 20 eccentric presses. Jürgen cuts out metal strips in lots of 2,000 and does other similar metal-cutting jobs.

The stupidity of his work is evident in the job description, too:

"The sheet metal is delivered from the warehouse and placed on blocks behind the plate shears at waist height. Adjust the machine, setting the stop fence at 90 ± 0.25. Take a sheet of metal from the pile, place it on the platform of the cutting machine, and make the first cut without running the sheet all the way over to the fence. Move the metal against the fence, cut the first strip, and check the width with the appropriate gauge. Readjust the fence setting if necessary.

"Continue shoving the sheet metal against the fence and cutting out strips. Place scrap metal in the special bin provided for it. The finished strips fall into a collecting rack placed behind the machine. Notify the shop mechanic if a burr begins to develop on the cut edges. Help the mechanic install a new knife in the machine. The shop transportation team is responsible for delivering the sheet metal and removing the racks and bins with finished strips and scrap metal in them. Notify this team as required.

"Maintenance of the machine (cleaning and greasing) is part of this job."

6 3   Jürgen is accustomed to seeing a job through from beginning to end. When he was working for Adolf, he figured out for himself what he would need in the way of materials and tools and then talked the job over with Adolf. When he was finished, he could see what he had done.

At Fahlbusch & Siebert he doesn't know what becomes of the sheet metal strips he cuts out or where they go when he's done with them. He never sees a finished product.

And on top of the apparent senselessness of his work comes the monotony of it. He goes through one complete work cycle every 55 seconds. Each sheet of metal produces 11 strips plus some scrap. The quota the job description sets is 100 strips every 8 minutes. But 8 minutes is not the amount of time Jürgen determines he needs to produce 100 strips. It is the amount of time management tells him he will take. Stress is thus added to senselessness and monotony. The result is even greater eruptions of anger after quitting time. Work is nothing but a vast, intolerable abyss in one's life.

Jürgen feels he is a captive in the factory, that he is completely subjected to others, that there is no possibility of liberation. It makes him furious that someone else can limit his freedom of movement, dictate to him how fast he has to work, when he can take a break, what he will do.

At the same time, he realizes the hopelessness of his situation. Any other job he might have at Fahlbusch & Siebert would be just as mindless and exhausting. He can't imagine that there is a single satisfying job in the whole firm.

He reacts the way he once did some years before, by turning his attention inward and subjecting his inner feelings and convulsions to elaborate self-observation. He spends hours at a time in the evening writing in his journal, describing his perceptions and emotions.

Within a few months, he has filled almost two hundred pages with raging tirades against his co-workers, the firm, the people on the trolley in the morning, society, the whole world.

Once again, Jürgen dreams of a world inhabited by him alone.

There is nothing in his diary about his job, the machines, the system that exploits him. Nothing about the positive side of work in a factory: the contact with others, learning what their lives are like, the sense of being strong together and working together to free oneself and others from inhuman working conditions, stress, exploitation.

All that counts for Jürgen are his feelings, his fears, and his sensibility.

He never wonders where those feelings come from. That other people might have similar feelings doesn't interest him. He doesn't know that collective fear can be defeated only by collective action. He feels entrapped in a social group that he perceives as a horde of mindless, unfeeling monsters, and he sees himself as the quintessential suffering creature.

He is a born artist.

After a few weeks, his desire for self-expression takes on a compulsive quality. He manifests his obsessions in seemingly insignificant observations that gain meaning only through his interpretation. That sensibility and pain have become ends in themselves is evident in the fact that Jürgen makes no connection between them and real events or experiences. This characteristic of his writing reveals itself in the mechanics of his style.

Jürgen distorts his sentence structure or changes tenses just so that he will be able to end a sentence with a word containing the vowels *a* or *i*. He is incapable of putting together any other kind of sentence. This produces some amusing and idiosyncratic writing, but it has the disadvantage of making Jürgen incapable of expressing some things in sentences at all.

·   ·   ·

As Jürgen turns more and more into himself, the few contacts he has are on the verge of dying out altogether.

Freddy talks to him about this. He talks about the meaning of work and the inextricable link between social, technological, and individual development. There can be no individual freedom, he says, unless human beings can liberate the forces of production, and this can happen only through the combined efforts of all the members of a society.

Once or twice a week in the locker room after work, Freddy asks, Shall we go have a beer?

Jürgen can't make much of Freddy's explanations. He doesn't particularly care why work in the plant is organized the way it is. All he wants is to step off the treadmill. He never sees the highly sophisticated technology that he supposedly helps create and that, as Freddy claims, represents progress for humanity. In his eyes, his job at Fahlbusch & Siebert is a step down from the good old days in Adolf's family business.

6 4   Jürgen's relationship with Freddy becomes more cordial only after Freddy does Jürgen a favor. Niebling is friendly with the firm's fire marshal.

The plant's fire squad consists of eight men who are broken down into two-man teams. Two men handle the nozzles at the site of the fire; two are responsible for the water supply; two others connect and lay the hoses. The last two act as mechanic and communications man. There is a first squad and a backup squad. Jürgen gets the job of water pumper on the backup squad.

The squads practice twice a week, working their way through every conceivable maneuver they might ever use in the plant. They set up the suction pump and lines, roll out the high-pressure hoses with a nice easy motion of the hand. The pumpers advance a second line to the left. Fire victims get rescued from pits and elevator shafts. Oil fires are smothered with foam. Rescues are made with the ladder truck. Everyone is trained in the proper use of the proper equipment: flashlights and replacement hoses, spray nozzles and hose patches.

The practice sessions are strenuous, but they get Jürgen away from the plate shears.

Since Fahlbusch has a number of outlying buildings and storehouses, the squads have to learn how to climb onto the right places on the fire truck in the right order.

Come on, Anton, move. We'd like to get on sometime, too.

Jürgen takes and passes, one after another, the basic course, the machinist's course, and the course on gas masks, air packs, and other protection against smoke inhalation.

Some of the classroom instruction is highly entertaining. One of the teachers, a man by the name of Stepputat, strikes Jürgen as being a pyromaniac. He explains what causes fires and explosions and how they spread.

Stepputat has a big box brought in. It contains all kinds of flammable materials along with devices and substances for putting fires out. Stepputat unpacks this box with the gestures of a magician. His demonstrations are good enough to be on TV. Every now and then, he has someone open a window to let the smoke and stench out. An assistant is standing by with a fire extinguisher, ready to step in whenever the fires that Stepputat sets on a big fireproof table look as though they might get out of hand.

Sometimes Stepputat's lectures turn into impromptu demonstrations on arson and the art of destroying buildings by fire. Using a small steel beam, he shows how heat causes steel to expand and lose its strength. At 500 degrees Celsius, a steel beam can carry only one half the load it can at normal temperatures; at 600 degrees only one third.

Thus, an intense fire in a room can cave in the ceilings of a steel-framed building and spread the fire to other floors. The expansion of the metal can even push out the side walls.

.   .   .

One of the gadgets Stepputat uses is a model stairwell with one wall made of fireproof glass.

With this model, Stepputat's students can actually see how gases and fires spread through a building. Later on, he demonstrates how water only intensifies some fires rather than putting them out.

In an interlude, he dips scraps of paper in some harmless-looking liquid and places them on ashtrays spread around in the classroom. After a few minutes, the pieces of paper spontaneously burst into flame.

Gases kept in pressurized containers are always potential sources of explosions, because gases double their volume if they are heated to 273 degrees.

If acetylene bottles are exposed to heat, the gas begins to break down, increasing the temperature and pressure inside the bottle tremendously.

Practically every metal worker or mechanic has welding gear in his workshop these days. The gas bottles are color-coded to indicate which gases they contain.

Jürgen is fascinated by all these new facts he is learning. He bores his friends in the Gasthaus zur Mitte with his questions.

What factors have to be present for combustion to take place?

By the time his vacation begins, Jürgen is a fully trained fireman who can set and extinguish any kind of fire.

6 5   At the end of June, 1974, the Schütrumpfs celebrate their silver anniversary. On this occasion, too, the party is small, and only close family friends are invited: Hans and Anni Mehlig with their daughter Ute; Erich and Hilde Schindewolf; Edith's brother Bübi with his wife, Gerda, and his daughter Christine. Christine is already married, also to a doctor, and has her daughter Manuela with her. Herbert sits next to Christine, Jürgen next to Ute. He would like to

stir up some trouble, but Edith has made him promise not to rub everyone's nose in the fact that he will be twenty-five in September.

The noon meal begins with a clear noodle soup. Next comes pork ribs with sauerkraut, boiled potatoes, and gravy. For dessert there is chocolate pudding topped with stewed pears. Jürgen and Herbert have put the leaves in the round living-room table and set the kitchen table next to it to make room for everyone.

Uncle Erich and Aunt Hilde have been there since late morning. Aunt Hilde is helping Edith with the cooking.

Adolf sings the blues: When you get old, nobody gives a damn what you think anymore. There are only three things anybody wants you to do: Hand over your cash, crawl on your belly, and croak.

Don't get so worked up, says Uncle Erich. That's the way it's always been with me.

There's a fight just before the other guests arrive. Adolf has had enough to drink, Edith says. With his liver. Adolf threatens to sabotage the party. I'll spill the beans on you. The whole world can know you're fooling around with that Frütrunk guy for all I care.

Oh, Adolf, just stop this nonsense, Edith says calmly. She adds apologetically: He's been acting a bit crazy lately. Aunt Hilde and Uncle Erich exchange a knowing glance. They can see that there's some truth to Adolf's accusation.

The party is no more eventful than any other celebration at the Schütrumpfs'. There are no effusive greetings. Everyone gets a brief hug from Edith. The guests are nervous about sinking into her soft flesh, but bulges spring back noiselessly to their original shape after the embrace. Only her eyes are slightly red. A tear runs down her right cheek. She has a talent for being moved on every occasion, genuinely moved. She's not putting it on for anyone's benefit. Except her own.

When they are seated at the table, the Mehligs are facing an oaken shelf with pewterware from a discount house on it. The Schindewolfs are placed so that they are looking at a large engraving of the orangery in K. that they gave Adolf for his fiftieth birthday.

If Mehlig looks up a little higher, he can see Adolf's pinup gallery, a collection of framed postcards depicting King Ludwig I of Bavaria's favorite mistresses. Among these postcards is an enlarged photograph of the Schütrumpfs and the Mehligs taken during the black-market days.

After the meal, the women wash up, make coffee, and cut the cakes. The kitchen is jammed full. Ute and Christine take Mehlig's dog for a walk. During this interlude, Adolf's dog is let out of the bathroom. He is always locked in whenever the Mehligs come because the two dogs don't get along. The men have a little drink.

Bübi is relieved to have found someone socially acceptable to talk to in Mehlig.

You belong to that fortunate generation that has never known anything but peace, says Mehlig. Abashed, Bübi lowers his eyes.

Jürgen knows what's coming. Sometime later in the evening, Mehlig will begin his old litany again: The German people have to be bathed in blood and tears from time to time. Otherwise they degenerate.

Being a farmer himself, Uncle Erich does not fall for that blood-and-soil stuff. As he usually does whenever he finds himself in the company of his betters, he plays the well-to-do trucking contractor who does a little farming on the side, almost as a hobby. Aunt Hilde, who does all the work, sits there with a strained smile on her face.

For the sake of form, the men drink a cup of coffee, then go back to their beer and schnapps.

At last something fit to drink after that tasteless brew. The conversation will not pick up noticeably until the alcohol concentration in the blood has reached 1.5 parts per one thousand. Then the women will have to exert a moderating influence.

·   ·   ·

About six o'clock, cold cuts and tea are served. Adolf keeps pressing beer and schnapps on his guests, but Bübi and Mehlig back off a bit. After the table is cleared, Adolf starts to get cantankerous.

Here we've been married for twenty-five years and just look how she's kicking up her heels now. You think you really know somebody after all those years, but then you find you've been deceived all along. He never would have believed it, but there it was.

This is the signal for the Mehligs and the Kreuzhackes to leave. Edith tries to keep them from going. Stay just a little longer. After they've left, she lashes out at Adolf: Well, you've managed to drive them away. I hope you're satisfied.

Then she says to Hilde: Come on, let's go sit in the kitchen. Good, Adolf growls, go sit in the kitchen where you belong, with the rest of the hired help.

In their separate chambers, the husbands and wives give vent to their feelings. Two hours later, Adolf and Erich are embracing each other and crying their hearts out.

Just look at those two sots, Aunt Hilde says.

She maneuvers her Erich out to the car and drives him home.

Jürgen and Herbert have gone to the Gasthaus zur Mitte hours ago.

6 6   This last summer puts a terrible strain on both partners in the marriage. Within only a few months, Edith has freed herself from Adolf's domination. The very first night after he is discharged from the hospital, Edith refuses to sleep in the same bed with him.

She sleeps on the living-room sofa for a few nights, but since she likes to go to bed early, Adolf can't feel free to watch television. So Edith takes over their marriage bed again, and from this point on Adolf sleeps in Herbert's bed, which is vacant because Herbert is away serving his tour of military duty. In the morning, before Jürgen goes to work, he looks at his father asleep in the boys' room. Adolf looks lost, fragile, almost as if he knows that everyone—himself included—has given up on him.

The next thing Edith does is get herself a job. She served an apprenticeship in retail sales from 1939 to 1942, then worked off and on as a typist until 1947. She readjusts to working life easily.

Adolf objects violently. He is seriously ill, he says, and needs care. If that's really true, Edith says, he's not a very convincing invalid.

Instead of taking care of himself, he started drinking again and eating all that greasy food just a few weeks after he was out of the hospital.

For the first time in his life, Adolf is left to his own devices during the day. He doesn't know what to do with himself.

He sits at the window for hours at a time without moving a muscle, as if everything he sees outside were dead. When the weather turns warmer, he spends a lot of time sitting in front of his garden shed in the yard. He is too weak to work. Defeated and resigned, he looks out over his little plot of land and the riverside park bordering it.

In better days, nothing could stop him until he had turned over the whole garden, raked it, and seeded it. He was constantly weeding and sowing new rows of radishes and lettuce. When summer comes, he brings his bedding out to the shed and sleeps on an old army cot. He has Jürgen bring him the camping stove, a propane bottle, and the portable TV.

By the time Edith and Jürgen get home from work in the evening, he has usually made his supper already, some indescribable slop swimming in grease and dotted with clumps of meat. He dumps his chamber pot in a ditch back by the fence. It's too much trouble to climb three flights of stairs whenever he has to go to the bathroom.

He used to criticize his sons if they didn't dress decently and were sloppy in their grooming. He felt nothing but disgust for the tramps that sneaked out of the park along the river early in the morning to avoid run-ins with the park staff. Now he looks like a derelict himself.

He has lost weight. His clothes hang on his flabby limbs. His fly is either open or buttoned up wrong. His pant legs are sprinkled with urine. His jacket and sweater are daubed with spilled food. He's usually unshaven. Dried saliva forms a yellowish crust in the corners of his mouth.

When Adolf is finally on his deathbed, Herbert criticizes his mother for not taking good enough care of him. Adolf could still be alive, Herbert claims, if Edith had kept him to his diet and shown more concern for him.

You're carrying on as if he were already dead, Edith says. They were all secretly wishing he would die, Jürgen says. As long as he was still alive, they all had to take him and his wishes into consideration.

6 7   It's true that Edith begins to go her own way once Adolf is too sick to force his will on her anymore.

Everybody lets him feel that he is near death. Poor Daddy, Jürgen says. I'm so glad that you're still alive at least.

Jürgen wants to give him a shave. Adolf resists.

You changed my diapers when I was a baby. I don't see why I shouldn't shave you now. Adolf gives in grudgingly.

Jürgen sets about his work lovingly and carefully. He washes the corners of Adolf's mouth with cotton and warm water. Adolf shoves him away with a resigned gesture. Never mind, son. It's no use anymore.

Edith professes gratitude as her motive for going to work. He worked for her for twenty-five years while she stayed at home. Now he can stay home, and she'll work for him. She owes him that.

During the week, Herbert is in Schwarzenborn, where there is a big army base. The troops call it "Blackborn City." They carry rolled-up tape measures in their pockets and cut off a centimeter every day.

Herbert comes home on weekends. You shouldn't be sad, Father. Haven't you had it good in life? You've lived your life. Life and death go together. We all have to die sometime.

Around Easter, Edith starts going out in the evening. Two nights a week, she goes to a course in bookkeeping. Once a week, she goes bowling.

Adolf gets suspicious. He thinks she is having an affair with Dr. Frütrunk, the family dentist.

After work, Edith sometimes lets a colleague named Faulstich walk her home. From his garden shed, Adolf sees them coming through the park. They stroll along slowly and seem to be engaged in conversation. In a few places, the path is hidden from view by trees and bushes.

When Edith comes home one evening, she realizes he has been drinking heavily. She can hear him screaming and yelling before she even reaches the house.

He bellows his accusations and suspicions at her across the yard. She's letting him go to the dogs while she runs around with other men.

Edith threatens to move out. That puts an end to Adolf's displays of jealousy and rage.

Edith's new independence from Adolf transforms her. Within a matter of weeks, she loses almost forty pounds and has to get new clothes. She buys her clothes alone now and with her own money. Adolf is insulted by this. At first he tries to make her deposit her salary in the family account that only he is authorized to draw on.

Edith insists on opening her own account, and Adolf interprets this as yet another insult.

Edith's appearance has changed dramatically. She wears makeup, she wears youthful clothes, and she bleaches her hair.

· · ·

Things come to a head in midsummer. Edith wants to go on vacation with two women friends. Adolf refuses to talk to her anymore unless she gives up this plan.

Both parents try secretly to enlist their sons' support. Herbert sides with Adolf. Jürgen remains neutral.

Edith sticks to her guns. On the morning of her departure, she goes out to the garden shed. Adolf totters out through the door.

I just wanted to let you know I'm going now.

Don't bother coming back.

A week later, when Jürgen comes home from work, Adolf is gone. In a panic, he calls Herbert.

He's old enough to take care of himself, Herbert says. The next morning at work, Bach Hein tells Jürgen there's a phone call for him. It's Edith. Adolf is with her.

Jürgen should come and pick him up.

Jürgen takes the rest of the day off to make the trip. Edith is vacationing in a pleasant resort town in the hill country of Hesse. The owner of the inn where Edith is staying tells Jürgen to look for her at a nearby café.

Edith is holding court at the table like some grande dame and busily conversing with her two companions. One is a physical-education teacher; the other a librarian. Neither of them is married.

Adolf is sitting next to her, slumped down in his chair but looking content.

Well, just look who's here, Edith calls out.

Who? Adolf asks quietly.

Our Jürgen.

Where?

Jürgen is introduced to the two ladies and offered a chair. I can't see, Adolf says.

I'm here, right next to you.

Oh, there.

They drive home that same evening. Adolf is very quiet.

I don't know if you can understand, he says, but I was afraid I would never see her again.

It was strange, Jürgen says. The minute he set foot in the inn and asked if his wife was there, he suddenly went blind.

After that they never quarreled again, not even after Edith came back from her vacation.

When they get home, Adolf refuses to sleep in the apartment and has Jürgen lead him out to his shed. Jürgen checks on him the next morning before going to work.

Adolf is sitting in front of the shed, looking straight into the rising sun.

When I was still a boy, he says, I saw the sun right in front of me every morning when I went to school.

Don't take me to the hospital if I get really sick again.

Just put me in a lawn chair so that I can see the sun rise.

6 8 In mid-August, shortly after Edith's return, Jürgen takes a trip to Sardinia. He has three weeks' vacation. The dockworkers in Genoa are on strike. He heads farther south along the Via Aurelia to Civitavecchia. He is in a rotten state of mind. The crisis in his parents' marriage troubled him a lot, he says. Two people live together for twenty-five years, and you think they're even happy in their own way.

Then suddenly you find out they haven't loved each other for ages. All they've been doing is hurting each other, and they can't say themselves why they've stuck it out together for so long.

Life turns out to be nothing but a series of accidental and usually wrong decisions that nobody has the courage to reverse. Jürgen feels sorry for Adolf. At the same time, he admires Edith because she had the guts to break away from Adolf and start a new life of her own.

I ask him what this new life of hers consisted of.

That didn't matter. What counts is that she managed to free herself from Adolf while he was still alive.

On Tuesday, August 20, he arrives in Golfo Aranci. He has spent the night on deck because all the cabins and deck chairs were already taken. He caught a few hours' sleep wrapped in a blanket and huddled in a sheltered corner. Most of the time he stared at the water.

It is just beginning to get light when he sees some dark clouds rise out of the sea off the bow. As the boat moves closer to them, Jürgen sees that they are rocky islands.

He makes a tour of the auto deck. Dirty bed linen is piled up in the passageways. People are crowded around the two bars. There's a smell of coffee in the air. The lounge is packed with people. Most of them look gray and bleary-eyed. Children are crying, husbands and wives snapping at each other. Jürgen can't understand a word but still has the feeling that he's understanding everything.

The harbor lies at the end of a long bay. It's broad daylight by the time the boat comes in to dock. The passengers stand elbow to elbow at the railing. There are only a few people on shore. Some of them wave.

As the boat puts in at the dock, the ship's crew knocks the blocks out from under the car wheels on the auto deck. The passengers shove and push and stampede to disembark. Jürgen feels that he is coming home. Later, he will often have the feeling that he lived on this island hundreds of years ago in a former existence.

He starts driving without looking at a map.

After traveling a few kilometers, he stops at a bay rimmed with rocks and goes swimming. There's not a soul to be seen.

Then he stretches out on a smooth rock above the water and falls asleep.

·　　·　　·

Just before he wakes up, he has a dream he has often had before. It is one of the three main dreams of his life. As a child, he used to dream he was being pursued by people who wanted to kill him.

He often stands as though glued to the spot and can't run away. Sometime he manages to run, but his feet are so heavy that he can hardly budge.

If he succeeds in running, his escape ends at the edge of a chasm. He can hear the murderers raging behind him. He has no choice. He has to jump. He wakes up in mid-leap before he hits the ground.

When he has this dream in later years, he knows that all he has to do to wake up and escape his murderers is jump.

As an adolescent, he dreams that he can fly. All he has to do is spread out his arms and move them up and down like wings. Even though he is sure he has flown many times before, he is frequently unable to raise himself off the ground. He takes a running start and flaps his arms until he finally takes off. He mustn't think about his belly and ribs. The minute he does, he can feel them scraping along on the ground. Then he realizes that he's skimming along only a few centimeters above the earth.

Sometimes he manages to rise up above the rooftops. But then he runs into another problem. There are power lines strung over the roofs. The sky is full of them. He has to try to find a place where he can fly between them without injuring himself.

In recent years, he has been dreaming he has to go somewhere by train. He keeps missing the train, or else he catches it only at the very last minute.

He usually has too much luggage, or his suitcases are too heavy.

As he sleeps on the rock above the sea near Porto Aranci, he can see the train station. It is surrounded by factories, freight yards, and apartment buildings, but there is no route through them to the station. His train will be leaving any minute now. He goes around the apartment block, getting farther and farther away from the station all the time.

When he wakes up, he is sitting in a train compartment. The train is moving through a narrow valley with wooded hills on either side. The area looks familiar to him. He suddenly realizes that he has to change trains in Bebra. The train is already pulling into the station. He's glad that he has only a light bag and his toilet kit with him.

He makes a final check of the luggage rack. It's piled high with books, sheet music, and manuscripts. The train has stopped already. He can hear the loudspeaker in the station. His penis begins to throb, and he has an erection.

He hurriedly tries to gather together his things from the luggage rack. He feels an ejaculation coming on. He piles the books and music onto his left arm. His arm can't carry any more, but there are still papers left on the rack. The loudspeaker requests the passengers to close the doors and wishes them a pleasant trip.

For a moment, he considers just dropping everything and leaping off the train. Then he continues taking things off the rack. His sexual excitement is extreme now. When the train begins to move again, he has an ejaculation. He immediately wakes up for the second time. He looks down at himself and feels his penis. It is limp and dry.

6 9   Jürgen spends the next few days driving all over the northern half of the island. He travels along the eastern coast, with its fancy hotels and villas, then along the poorer Spanish west coast. In the north, he walks for hours at a time through the old run-down sections of town in the center of Sassari. They strike him as much more human than the faceless tracts of new buildings in K.

He also explores the interior of the island. The minute anything catches his attention—a pile of stones in a field, a castle ruin on a hilltop above a dilapidated village—he stops. The leisurely pace and aimlessness of his journey are relaxing and soothing to him. For the first time in his life, he is capable of meeting people openly, without projecting his expectations onto them. He is able to listen to them and learn from them.

He is lucky. Inland from Oristano, on the west coast about halfway down the island, he picks up a girl hitchhiking. She wants to go to Nuoro, toward the northeast. He is heading south.

Where are you going? he asks.

Are you going anywhere near Nuoro?

Hop in.

All at once he realizes how aimless his travels are.

She is in her early to mid-twenties. Her face with its prominent cheekbones has something old-fashioned about it. She has brown eyes and chestnut-brown hair. She is wearing dark brown slacks of lightweight corduroy, hiking shoes of soft leather with a heavy crêpe rubber sole, a plaid flannel shirt. She carries an olive-green windbreaker slung over her arm. The only luggage she has is a canvas tote bag. Her German is grammatically perfect, but she speaks with a heavy accent.

The girls Jürgen knows at home want to be entertained and have nothing to say themselves. You always have to watch out that you don't say the wrong thing.

Giovanna Tolu is talkative. Without much encouragement at all, she tells Jürgen about her family and herself. One small question is enough to set her off. Jürgen lets her talk. He has the idea that she's pleased finally to be able to use the language she is studying.

She keeps asking him: Did I say that right?

Jürgen corrects her in a good-natured way. Halfway to Nuoro they stop in a village to eat. Jürgen treats her.

When they arrive in Nuoro after three or four hours, Jürgen knows quite a bit about her, her family, and life on Sardinia.

·　　·　　·

Her parents come from the village of Orgosolo near Nuoro. When Giovanna was three, the police staged a large raid on her village.

The ostensible reason for the raid was to crack down on bandits and their accomplices. But the raid was really directed against Communists, union members, and separatists.

There are police raids like this every few years, she says.

Her family had a small farm. Her father is a Communist and a leader in the local union. He was arrested along with a few dozen other men and women. Some of them were tried and sentenced.

Most of them were released after a few months. Giovanna's father was banned from Sardinia and sent to the Italian mainland for several years. His wife and children went with him. When his term of exile was over, Lorenzo Tolu decided to settle in Rome and run a newspaper stand in Tiburtina I, the workers' quarter right next to the offices of the Communist Party newspaper *L'Unità*.

Giovanna attended a secondary school in Rome and is now in her tenth semester at the university. She is studying Germanic languages and history. Her major subjects are English and German. She is planning to go to England for a year soon, then to the Federal Republic, to perfect her languages.

Once a year, the Tolu family goes to Orgosolo to visit their friends and relatives. On these visits, Giovanna doesn't get a chance to see the island. Most Sardinians never travel beyond the narrow confines of their villages.

This is the first time that Giovanna has traveled around the island by herself.

Her native country is a surprise to her. The island is made up of many self-contained regions, with their own dialects, their special social and legal norms, and their own cultural histories. Even the geographic and economic differences are striking.

She is planning to explore the mountainous interior of the island during the next few days. She usually travels by bus, but sometimes she hitchhikes, too, because the buses run infrequently and the connections are poor.

Jürgen is bowled over. Giovanna is full of stories about this island, which seems as new to her as it is to him.

The scientific thoroughness she brings to the study of her homeland is something new for him. He can't imagine that anyone would ever be moved to travel through West Germany this way and study its peoples and regions. Almost like an anthropologist coming to a strange and unexplored country.

At the same time, he realizes how little he knows about his own native country.

He has the impression that Giovanna knows more about Germany than he does. Her political ideas strike him as way out of line. As far as politics was concerned, she was worse than a Communist, he says.

She calls the Federal Republic an American satellite. His country's main mission was to promote and carry out American policy in Europe. The fact that the American Secretary of State calls West Germany the most loyal ally of the United States makes that quite obvious.

The leading politicians in West Germany were nothing but errand boys for the United States. The first thing they did after the war was sabotage the development of a self-sufficient Germany and make West Germany totally dependent on America.

The present division of Germany can be laid primarily to the machinations of West German politicians from all the major parties. The West Germans sold their national independence for a few dollars.

This is why the leading SPD and CDU politicians set out to crush Socialist and Communist movements in Germany from the very beginning. What the Federal Republic needs, she says, is a strong Communist Party and a union movement that represents a real threat to big business, as it does in Italy, and that will fight for Socialism.

7 0   The calm and gentle way in which she expresses her opinions confuses Jürgen. In the Federal Republic, women Communists are depicted as sexless, fanatic gun molls devoid of feelings and charm.

But Jürgen finds Giovanna extremely attractive and feminine despite her boyish clothes.

What surprises him most is her knowledge of German culture. She has studied the classical philosopers and writers of the eighteenth and nineteenth centuries. At first he tries to put her in her place with his spotty knowledge. But she knows more than he does and counters his arguments with quotes and detailed information.

When he brings the conversation around to music and tells her something about Richard Wagner, he finds that she is well informed in this field, too. Jürgen doesn't know what to make of all this. Here is a Communist who admires Beethoven and Mozart, quotes German philosophers, and has read Brecht's plays in the original.

Jürgen doesn't know any Brecht except for a few songs from *The Threepenny Opera*. Giovanna asks if there is a theater in K., if Brecht's plays are staged there often, if Jürgen goes to the theater a lot, if he has seen the new German films. A few years ago, a movie house in Rome ran nothing but German films for several weeks.

Jürgen squirms, makes excuses. This conversation with her is embarrassing for him.

At the same time, he is proud that such an intelligent and well-educated girl is talking to him as though he were an equal.

Jürgen falls back on his talent for adapting himself to other people. He represents himself as a progressive and class-conscious young worker who has large gaps in his education because of the discrimination inherent in the German educational system. He claims he is active as an unpaid volunteer in the union movement.

He rails against the exploitation practiced in his country, drawing on expressions he has heard from Freddy. He tells her about Freddy and Konrad, and claims that the three of them make up a Communist cell in the factory.

He says that his true allegiance is to the German Democratic Republic, but you can't admit to that publicly in West Germany.

To his surprise, she responds coolly to this. Her party recognizes that great social progress has been made in the GDR. But there are certain things about the GDR that she cannot accept.

Then I asked her what party she was in, Jürgen says. And she said she belonged to the Communist Party. Can you make any sense out of that?

7 1   At the bus terminal in Nuoro, Giovanna asks Jürgen if he wouldn't like to go to Orgosolo with her.

For a moment he is overcome by his old fear of the unfamiliar. He is afraid of getting to know new people or going into a bar where he has never been before. Sometimes he broods for weeks before he can decide to go into a bar or approach someone.

His love for Giovanna gets him over this fear, and he drives to the mountain village.

Giovanna's parents and her little brother are staying with Lorenzo's brother Saverio Tolu. Giovanna and her younger sister sleep in the kitchen of a neighbor named Olga Pittui. Her husband and his brother are working in the Federal Republic. Giovanna says: They are emigrants.

The only hotel in the town is completely filled up. Most of the guests are Sardinians who are working abroad and have come home on their vacations to visit relatives. About 700,000 Sardinians live and work abroad, 400,000 of them in Italy, 270,000 in other European countries, and 30,000 in non-European countries.

In other words, one third of the Sardinian population does not live on Sardinia.

Giovanna takes Jürgen to a Signora Manca. She is a small but matronly old woman whom everyone in Orgosolo knows. At one time or another, various members of her family have been suspected of being bandits or of collaborating with them.

In Vittorio de Seta's film *The Bandits of Orgosolo*, Signora Manca plays the old matriarch who, together with the other women, bakes paper-thin Sardinian bread.

Giovanna talks with her. It seems she doesn't want to give Jürgen a place to sleep. Some women from the neighborhood have stopped by to see what's going on.

They wear long black skirts and large black or brown shawls. Some of the shawls are colorfully embroidered. When the women go out on the street, they pull the shawls up over their heads and cover the lower part of their faces, leaving only their eyes exposed.

The conversation lasts almost an hour.

Jürgen is completely calm now. He has the feeling that nothing bad can happen to him on this island.

Later, Signora Manca leads him into a small room that has a separate entrance. This is where her daughters used to sleep, Giovanna explains.

Little by little, Jürgen learns something about the village. Orgosolo has always been regarded as the headquarters of the bandits who operate in this region. Most of its inhabitants have had run-ins with the authorities sometime in the past. Police cruisers and jeeps patrol all the roads leading into town.

In 1954, the magazine *Nuovi Argomenti* published a detailed study of the village written by Franco Cagnetta. A French translation appeared in 1963; and in 1964, Econ published it in the Federal Republic under the title *The Bandits of Orgosolo*.

A number of other publications about the town followed. No other

Sardinian village has ever received so much publicity. When the Italian authorities become irate, this is where they strike first. But this is also the village where resistance against state tyranny and abuse of power is strongest.

Everywhere in Orgosolo and in the neighboring villages slogans are written on the walls: Sardinia for the Sardinians! Down with colonialism in Sardinia! Long live the Sardinian People's Republic! Long live the free people of Sardinia!

The idea of Sardinian independence and the sense that Sardinia is a separate nation with its own history, language, and culture are most alive in the mountain regions of the island.

Here old Sardinian law remains as a system of norms that continues to vie with the legal system imposed by the Italian conquerors.

7 2   Because of the isolation of these mountain villages, the music, too, does not seem to have changed for centuries. The shepherds of Barbagia, as the region around Orgosolo is called, have a unique singing style. When we went to Orgosolo last year to interview Giovanna, we heard strange sounds emanating from a tavern the first night we were there. The room was full of shepherds. It smelled of cheese, leather, and sweat.

The sounds we had been unable to identify turned out to be singing.

The words are sung by a soloist, accompanied by a chorus of three men. After each verse of the song, which is more of a recitative, the chorus sings a few long-drawn-out chords.

The voices in the chorus sound like primitive instruments that seem to imitate the bleating of sheep. The men create this sound by holding one hand alongside their mouths, the other behind one ear, and leaning their heads together.

·   ·   ·

Later on, two shepherds sit down in front of a table and take turns singing. One is large and fat, the other small and thin. We can't understand a word. Giovanna explains the song to us. The two shepherds are poets who are improvising. After every verse, the chorus sings a cadence. In strophe and antistrophe, the two poets debate a subject that a guest has set for them. A well-argued point draws applause.

The two poets are as different as night and day. The fat one acts sure of himself and sings with a poker face. His only show of feeling is an occasional angry glance cast at his opponent. He sits quietly and appears to be deep in concentration. The small man seems to rely on gestures and comic facial expressions to make up for what he lacks in poetic powers and rigor. We like the small man better, but the aficionados in the tavern prefer the fat one.

There are a lot of lay poets in Sardinia, most of them shepherds and farmers. At holiday festivals there is often a singing contest. The themes and the names of the contestants are publicized on posters. The verses the poets make up in these competitions are privately published later and offered for sale. On the edge of the festival grounds there is a stand that sells poems by participants in the day's contest. The texts, which are almost always printed at the poet's own expense, usually appear on single sheets or, sometimes, in brochures.

We ask the two poets if we can tape-record their performance. The fat man immediately orders a round of red wine for everyone. The poets want to take the nature of poetry as their theme for this contest, a theme that Sardinian poets—like poets anywhere—are much given to debating.

For a long time, their song focuses on who we really are, where we might come from, and whether it's worth their trouble to perform for us at all. The smaller man seems to be arguing against us; the fat man is for us. He thinks it clever of us to make a tape recording.

·　·　·

Finally they come to their chosen subject.

Their debate is sprinkled with asides in which they accuse each other of stupidity, incompetence, and lack of poetic talent. Their singing dialogue lasts for two hours. Then the tavern owner throws everybody out.

Outside, the fat man tells us that the little man is not a good poet. He complains about the dearth of good poets these days. It used to be that you'd find a couple of good poets in every tavern. It was really fun to sing with people like that. Nowadays you can go from one tavern to another night after night and never find a decent poet. So you wind up singing with dilettantes like this guy tonight.

It's one o'clock in the morning. The twenty-odd people that are standing in front of the tavern with us want to hear the tape. They listen attentively and once again express their approval or disapproval at certain passages.

The fat man moves his lips as though he were repeating every word. Just before the song ends, the machine runs out of tape. There wasn't enough to record the whole session. Now the fat man is angry. He starts cursing.

The others try to calm him down. He turns away angrily to leave. We call after him and apologize for the error.

He raises his hand in a gesture of regal magnanimity and says in Italian: Please! Don't give it another thought. There are plenty more words where those came from—and every bit as good.

7 3   One time when I'm visiting Jürgen in prison in W., I ask him whether he heard this strange music when he was in Orgosolo.

I can see that my question revives the profound impression this music made on him. But he rejects my use of the adjective "strange."

He says he can't imagine that any music could come more directly from the vital heart of a whole people than this music does. It is not the product just of individual artists.

Compared to music like that, all the highly cultivated music of Europe was pure garbage.

He stays only a few days with Giovanna in Orgosolo. Then he joins her on a tour through Barbagia. The account of this trip is Giovanna's.

The first thing they did was visit a cousin of her father's who lives in Baunei but spends most of the year tending his sheep in the hills. Giovanna's uncle gives them detailed directions on how to reach his hut.

On the road to Baunei, an older man flags Jürgen down and asks for a ride. He is wearing clothes typical of Sardinian shepherds: a dark, heavy corduroy suit, a small peaked cap, ankle-high shoes, and leather leggings. He is carrying a large goatskin sack over his shoulder. He never went to school and speaks only Sardinian. He has never been on the Italian mainland.

When Giovanna and Jürgen are about to drop him off at his house, he invites them in.

For Jürgen, this unexpected hospitality, devoid of all ulterior motives, adds support to his feeling that he has stumbled into a paradise.

You know how people are in our country, he says. They hide their wurst when company's coming.

The man's wife is thirty; he is fifty-nine. The house is tiny. It has only a large kitchen, a small bedroom, and a number of storerooms.

The woman brings wine, goat cheese, and *carta da musica*, as the paper-thin, crumbly Sardinian bread is called. The man watches her, winks, and says: I'd forgotten up there in the mountains that women even existed. They have been married only a few years.

Now he has leased some pastureland near the village and comes home every day. At five in the morning, he has half a liter of red wine, a few raw eggs, and a thick slice of bacon for breakfast.

He keeps lots of food stored in the house.

The mice have been nibbling at the fifty-odd goat cheeses, nearly black, that he has in the cellar. There are chunks of rather unappetizing pork, smoked and salted, lying around. Even the pig's head is split and pickled. There are pigs' ears in an old stoneware crock.

They have a homemade schnapps with the meal. Stuffed with food and half drunk, they step out into the harsh light. In the car, Giovanna passes on to Jürgen everything the man has told her. She is less enthusiastic than Jürgen. She says he is wrong in seeing the intolerable hygienic conditions and the primitive way of life that is forced on these people as evidence of an intact unity of life, work, and environment.

7 4   As they are nearing the turnoff that leads to her relative's *ovile*, a drove of pigs crosses the road. The pigs are smaller and shorter-bodied than the German breeds, but they have long legs and are more mobile. Suddenly the brush on every side is swarming with pigs, pigs, and more pigs. There are goats and sheep grazing among the rocks, too.

But where are the shepherds?

A bit farther ahead, there is a dirt road going off to one side. This must be the place.

They drive about ten kilometers into the mountains. The road is wretched. Brooks run across it in some places. Flocks of sheep, goats, and pigs block their way continually. A few water buffalo are grazing alongside the road. Occasionally they see a donkey or a horse, too.

Jürgen is happy.

He felt like an explorer in a strange land, Giovanna says.

The road ends at a large rock. A tin can is hanging on a twisted tree to the left. On the light-colored rock they can see a dirt-brown footpath leading into the mountains. They hesitate for a moment, then start to follow it. Half an hour later, they hear dogs barking in the distance. They suddenly find themselves in a small rock basin. Now they realize that the tin can was a signpost.

· · ·

They see a hut standing under two large oaks at the edge of the basin. That is the *ovile*, from *ovini*, the word for sheep. In the open area in front of the hut are two round corrals that look almost prehistoric. They are built of rocks piled up without mortar. Whitish weathered tree branches are stuck in the rock walls to form a thick fence about two meters high. The sheep and goats are herded into these corrals for the night. Copper kettles for cheese making hang on the trees in front of the *ovile*.

The shepherd calls his dogs in. He is standing in front of the *ovile*, leaning on his rifle, and he invites us to come inside.

The room is full of smoke. A heavy log is burning in the middle of it. Gradually our eyes get accustomed to the darkness. A rack hanging from the ceiling has cheeses on it that are being dried and browned in the smoke. There are two pallets in a corner.

Giovanna finally introduces herself and her companion. It takes a little while for the man to understand who she is. He has seen her only once in his life, and that was at her baptism. He sees her uncle in Orgosolo more often. It's a shame that Giovanna's father has to live in Italy.

They both bemoan the fate of Sardinia, which hasn't been able to support its own children ever since the Piedmontese took it over.

Giovanna sends Jürgen to get the bottle of aquavit from the bag they have left outside the hut. Sebastiano Puiole gets out three paper cups and pours drinks. Later he rinses out the cups and offers them some of his red wine. He keeps his water and wine in plastic containers. They clash with some traditional utensils he has. Sardinian shepherds have been whittling similar utensils out of suitable pieces of wood for millennia.

Uncle Sebastiano owns a vineyard, which his wife tends. She and their four children live down in the village about thirty kilometers from here. Uncle Sebastiano and the other shepherd living with him take turns going to the village once a week to take the cheese down and bring supplies back up. They used to use a donkey for this, but now that there's a road, they drive a Fiat 500. Whatever meat they need, they slaughter themselves. Sometimes they shoot a wild boar or a few partridge.

They spend their summers up here in the mountains without television, newspapers, taverns, friends.

During the winter months, they lease pastureland in a desolate area on the coast where they are just as isolated as they are here. They pay their lease in kind, mostly with cheese but sometimes with a few sheep or goats as well.

He offers them something to eat. The cheese is full of maggots that make it crumbly and sharp. Nobody knows whether the maggots are in the cheese because of the lack of hygiene or because they make it taste better. He dunks his *carta da musica* in wine to soften it because his teeth are bad.

Then he describes how the cheese is made. They milk from April through July. Their flock consists of about 200 goats and sheep that produce some 40 pounds of cheese a day. That adds up to over 5,000 pounds of cheese a year, worth about 20,000 marks.

Giovanna asks him if he likes being a shepherd.

No. It doesn't pay anymore. It costs too much to support his family.

He lists many other reasons: the isolation, the loneliness, the primitive living conditions. Many shepherds have skin diseases and worms. The amount of work is way out of proportion to the returns. And there is social discrimination, too. Shepherds are the lowest of the low. Sometimes a squad of carabinieri descends on the *ovile* and interrogates him for hours at a time.

But he has no choice. He has been living in the mountains as a shepherd since he was six.

The dogs start barking. A young man appears in front of the hut. He has a rifle on his shoulder. He is Sebastiano's neighbor. The pasturage that he and his brother lease lies a few kilometers inland. He is looking for his animals. During a storm, it's hard to keep them together because you can't hear their bells.

The animals often get lost or fall into crevices in the rocks. Foxes, birds of prey, and rustlers are also a threat to the herd.

But the weather is the greatest enemy. This year is so dry that the sheep and goats are eating the bark off the trees. The pigs won't put on any weight because there won't be any acorns for them to eat in the fall. In years like this, some shepherds will have to sell their flocks to be able to pay their leases.

Come back again when the weather's good, Puiole says as his guests leave. We'll slaughter a lamb and have a party. We're always here. We've got plenty of time.

7 5   Jürgen sits there and sinks into a reverie.

He feels safe and secure. The shepherd's hut is like a memory of some time far in the past when the meaning of life was still inherent in the process of living.

The frame of the *ovile* is built of beams set in stone postholes. The walls are made of rough boards. Overhead there is a loft floored with planks, laid side by side with gaps between them. The cheeses lie on the planks, and the smoke escapes through a hole in the ceiling. Jürgen would have loved to have had such a hut when he was a child.

There are some things on the island that set Jürgen to thinking about other times in which he would have liked to live, things like the nuraghi, for example. They are huge round towers in various stages of decay, towers built by a people said to have come to Sardinia by way of Cyprus and Egypt. These strange towers, which squat in the middle of the fields like symbols of a bygone age, have cyclopean walls that are a meter thick and rise up to form domed roofs. At the top there is a smokehole just like the one in Uncle Sebastiano's hut.

What kind of dialect is this that the people speak here? Jürgen asks.

It's no dialect, Giovanna says. It's Sardinian. It's a separate language.

How come you can talk to your uncle, then?
I grew up speaking Sardinian at home.
Even in Rome?

Jürgen imagines that Hessian is his native language and that people at home speak Hessian, not German.

In Fonni, the highest village on Sardinia, they ask directions to the house where Bacchisio Falconi used to live. He was a famous bandit in the thirties and forties. He was born in 1906, and in 1936 he was convicted of shooting a carabiniere and sentenced to thirty years of hard labor. He escaped and fled into the mountains above Fonni. A carabiniere shot him in 1949.

A young man takes them to his widow's house. She asks them to come back a little later.

When they return in an hour, she invites them into her little kitchen. She never went to school, and speaks Italian poorly. "Any child speaks it better than I do," she says. "They start learning it right off in school."

When Giovanna inquires about Bacchisio, the old woman asks if Giovanna can give her any money. Giovanna gives her 3,000 lire.

Then the woman leads her visitors into a second-floor bedroom where she keeps cheese, ham, and sacks of chicken feed. The room is darkened and packed full.

On the dresser there is a photograph of Falconi leaning on his rifle. After a while, the old woman takes a pamphlet out of a drawer in the sewing machine.

Back in the kitchen, she asks Giovanna to read the title page out loud. Giovanna reads:

A Sardinian song about the great misfortune that befell Bacchisio Falconi, son of Giovanni from Fonni, written by Falconi himself. One hundred and twenty stanzas of eight lines each, written in 1943, all of them rhyming.

Widow Falconi's idiot son, born in 1948, who has been squatting lethargically next to the fireplace, jumps up, whoops with joy, waves his arms around. The woman quiets him.

Giovanna has heard of this poem, and leafs through the pages. There was once an old woman selling private printings of Sardinian poems at the bus terminal in Nuoro. Falconi's poem was among them. The old woman wanted 2,000 lire for it, but Giovanna had been too stingy to pay that much.

Falconi's widow mumbles complaints under her breath as Giovanna reads in the pamphlet: "There she goes reading everything out of it, and when she's done she won't give me a red cent!"

In the years right after World War II, Falconi used to turn up at festivals and sing his poem. There was never any problem finding three men to make up the chorus. Giovanna wants to buy the pamphlet. The old woman swears that it's her last copy and asks 20,000 lire for it.

Giovanna puts the pamphlet back on the table. The old woman sinks into disappointed silence. After a while, she leans over to Giovanna and asks if she would like to buy some gold jewelry. Giovanna wouldn't. The old woman falls silent again. Suddenly she stands up and declares amiably that she'll make some coffee now. While she works, she tells about her life with Bacchisio. Every now and then, she reverts to her mumbled cursing and complaining.

While everyone is drinking coffee, Falconi's widow hands Giovanna the pamphlet and asks her to read aloud from it. The poem is written in Sardinian. Giovanna reads.

The old woman leans forward in her chair. Her eyes light up. She frequently nods her head and repeats a few sentences herself.

When Giovanna reads the passage where Falconi cries out that he, like Jesus Christ, is innocent of the crime he is being condemned for and calls his judge Pontius Pilate, the old woman's excitement rises even higher. "Yes!" she exclaims. "Innocent like Christ!"

Before Giovanna and Jürgen leave, she sells them a large goat cheese. They refuse the ham she wants to sell them. Giovanna has not gotten the poem.

On the return trip to Orgosolo, Giovanna and Jürgen happen onto one of the festivals that Falconi used to perform at. A few kilometers outside of Mamoiada there is a small church in an open field. A row of low houses stand around the church in a square. These buildings belong to the village and are administrated commonly by all the inhabitants. Once a year, a few hundred people come out here, stay for a week, and put on a festival.

All Sardinian festivals last a week.

The people who have rented the houses are sitting in front of them. Wine is being served in a few summerhouses. Outside the gate, tiny suckling pigs are being roasted over an open fire. A horse race is about to be held on a meadow. A few hundred people are waiting for the race to begin. The plants crushed under their feet give off a sweet aroma. It is hot.

Later on, the parade of the mamuthones takes place in front of the church. Some shepherds have blackened their faces. They wear fur masks on their heads. Their bodies are wrapped in heavy black pelts. They have tied a number of different-sized bells to their bodies with string. They stamp rhythmically and make an incredible racket.

In the evening the dancing begins. An accordion plays the same musical sequence over and over again for hours at a time. Partners link arms and form a circle, dancing one step forward and one to the side, but the couples never close the circle by joining hands all around.

Since Giovanna and Jürgen are the only strangers, everyone wants to buy them a drink and touch glasses with them, but no one will accept their offers to buy a round of drinks in return. Later on in the night, fires are lit and people start drinking schnapps. They get drunker still.

. . .

Along toward midnight there is a brawl. A few men have fought with knives. One of them is dead. He is the twenty-fourth victim of the famous *disamistade* of Mamoiada. A *disamistade*, also called a *faida*, is the private blood feud provided for in traditional Sardinian law.

This one began in 1953 with the termination of an engagement. That in itself was not sufficient cause for a *faida*.

Sexual morality is freer in Sardinia than it is in Calabria or Sicily. It is no disgrace for a girl to have had lovers before marriage. In traditional law there was no double standard for men and women.

The event that precipitated this *disamistade* took place in 1954 when the bride's family claimed that the groom's family had publicly accused them of having reported the theft of some cattle to the police. This report to the police violated the code of Barbagia because cattle theft was a punishable crime under Italian law but not under Barbagian law.

That is what sparked the vendetta.

7 6   Even today, Jürgen has to resort to metaphor when he tries to describe what his meeting with Giovanna meant to him.

It was like coming across a blue horse standing in a meadow. Like something in a dream. You find yourself walking down a street you've seen before in an earlier life.

He suddenly understands why his attempts to form friendships in the past had failed. They had all been directed toward some special end. They were flights from reality that were bound to fail. Being close to a girl meant fucking, nothing but fucking, grabbing her breasts, feeling her ass, kissing.

So we kissed, and we were so busy kissing that we forgot to ask:

What's your name? Who are you? What interests you? Shall I tell you something about me? What would you like to know? Tell me something about yourself and your interests.

We reduced all our feelings to the common denominator of sex, as if human beings consisted of nothing else. We couldn't sense anymore who the other person really was.

It wasn't any different with boys either. We always had to be doing something. Go have a beer, invent some kind of project, feel we were the greatest thing going.

Giovanna is different. Giovanna takes things in and gives back what she has taken in: her surroundings, the people she sees, the conditions of their lives. That's the way she functions. For her, everything has its significance. Jürgen strikes her as naïve, but she lays that to the fact that Sardinia is completely new to him. Her main reason for taking him along with her is not simply because he is a pleasant traveling companion. He is open to experience, asks questions, and stimulates her to ask questions she otherwise would never have thought to ask.

Then, too, he represents a certain protection for her. A woman traveling alone has to be always on her guard against men. She can't have a moment's peace; she will be pestered constantly. If she rebuffs them, they will curse her out: Old hag, lousy lesbian, can't find your cunt for the spiderwebs.

If she responds to a pass in a friendly way, then there is always the possibility that any reluctance she may show later on will be interpreted as prudish reserve that has to be broken down by force.

Jürgen doesn't make any passes.

This is a frequently recurring pattern in his behavior.

He experiences one sexual orgy after another in his daydreams, but when he is actually face to face with a woman, he is often so shy that he hardly dares to touch her.

·　　·　　·

He is also incapable of doing anything without imagining in advance how he wants it to be.

He imagines a relationship with Giovanna in which both partners can develop their personalities. The separate personalities they bring into the marriage will not remain static. The relationship will clearly change them both, but they will retain their distinct identities and enjoy equal status because he, the man, will not try to force the woman into a subordinate position and impose his will on her.

A relationship like this calls for a woman who is strong, secure in herself, and intelligent. In other words, Giovanna.

In their marriage, both partners will have their own jobs, their own friends, their own interests. What each partner has, he or she will bring into the relationship to the enrichment of the other.

They don't even need to marry. A common apartment is all that's necessary. They would both contribute to the household financially and both share in the housework.

There would always be the possibility of children, and their arrival would have to bring some changes.

She could not work anymore, and he would have to provide for her and the children.

He would have to work extra hours, perhaps do some moonlighting. And she could do all the housework alone now because she would have more time for it.

Her role would, of course, change. She would take on the role of a wife and mother whose main task is to care for her children. Her contribution to the marriage would consist of caring more lovingly than ever for her husband, doing the housework for him, and sharing his problems and worries.

All of sudden, in his mind's eye, Jürgen sees a photograph of his parents. They are sitting on a park bench in the sunshine, decked out in their Sunday best. Jürgen, still a small child, is standing on Adolf's lap. A baby carriage, presumably with Herbert in it, stands between Adolf and Edith.

Edith holds on to the bar of the carriage with one hand as if she is afraid it will roll away from her.

Jürgen has the feeling that he is nothing more than an empty physical shell in which his father has taken up residence. He claims he can feel the way his father sits and walks. This father figure inside him fills his entire body from head to toe, fills him so completely that he feels mentally and emotionally at one with his father.

In Orgosolo, Jürgen invites Giovanna to come with him to Germany and asks when it was she was planning to make her first trip abroad.

This September, she says. Jürgen says she can stay at his house when she first arrives.

They have only three rooms, but she could sleep in the living room.

Jürgen has been a guest in a number of Sardinian homes in the last few weeks.

It's a matter of course here that a guest be offered hospitality no matter how small or crowded a family's living quarters are.

Giovanna promises to think it over.

On Jürgen's last evening on Sardinia, she asks him to come to Signora Pittui's with her. He feels his insides freeze up. She wants to take him with her. She wants to sleep with him.

His newly aroused longings will be satisfied sooner than he ever expected. Here is a woman who doesn't have to be pursued, who doesn't have to be conquered, a woman who decides for herself when she wants to go to bed with a man, a woman who likes to make love a lot.

7 7   Signora Pittui receives her guest from Germania as if he were the king of Spain. Giovanna interprets. Signora Pittui asks where he would like to sit, if he would like something to eat, what he would like to drink.

Jürgen asks for a beer. Signora Pittui sends a young woman who is at her house to the nearest bar. Jürgen protests. He'll take whatever she has on hand. Too late. The young woman has already been shoved out the door. Signora Pittui comes back into the room with some bread and a ham she has just cut into.

She apologizes for the shabby impression her living room must make on him. As a German, he must be used to more comfortable and elegant living quarters. But she and her husband are saving every penny they earn. When he returns from Germany, they want to open a little pensione with a bar and restaurant somewhere on the coast, maybe in Arbatax.

She asked Giovanna to bring Jürgen over because he is leaving for Germany the next day. She would like him to take a letter along for her husband and mail it in Germany. The mail from Sardinia sometimes takes a week or longer.

Her husband is living with his brother, who is renting an apartment for himself and his family. It's not a very good apartment, and it's very expensive, but it's better than nothing.

Is it true that Germans don't like to rent to foreigners?

Jürgen finds this question very embarrassing. That's not true of his family. His father manages several apartment houses and has a number of foreign workers as tenants.

May I ask, he says, what city your husband is in?

Patricio Pittui and his brother Francesco work as metal workers for the same company.

In K.

In K.? I'm from K.

Then you must know the firm . . .

She says the name. Giovanna can't catch it.

The way Signora Pittui pronounces it makes it impossible to understand.

She digs in a dresser drawer for one of her husband's income statements. She has to present it to the town tax office. It's pure formality. Her husband used to be on the village council. She has taken over his seat now.

For which party? Jürgen asks.

Communist, of course, Giovanna answers.

Orgosolo has a Communist mayor.

The village governing board is made up of Communists, Socialists, members of the Sardinian separatist party, and two Christian Democrats.

Jürgen is amazed.

Communists, Social Democrats, and CDU all on the same governing board?

Giovanna can understand his surprise. The Italians know that members and sympathizers of the German Communist Party are denigrated and persecuted in the Federal Republic.

That's one of the reasons why she wants to go to Germany.

If you come from a country with a strong Communist Party and are a Communist, you want to see for yourself if a country where Communists are persecuted the way witches were in the Middle Ages is capable of any kind of progress. You want to learn firsthand whether democracy, a free press, and freedom of speech are possible there at all.

Jürgen is apologetic. He has nothing against Communists himself. He tries to explain why most of his countrymen oppose Communism. As he talks, he realizes how little he knows about Communists. Ill at ease, he resorts to the arguments he has picked up from television, the newspapers, his teachers and parents, his friends and acquaintances. He suddenly finds them unconvincing because he realizes Giovanna does not find them convincing.

He lowers his eyes and looks at the income statement. Patricio works for Fahlbusch & Siebert. Signora Pittui is delighted. Then you must know him. Francesco works there, too. Jürgen doesn't know either one of them.

Of course, he says. Francesco and Patricio. I know them well, but only by their first names.

How is Patricio? What kind of work does he do?

Fine. He's fine. At least he was before I left on vacation.

What does he do in the factory?

I don't know. He's in a different section.

Giovanna kisses him on both cheeks when he leaves the next day. She puts her arms around him. He can feel what large breasts she has. He pulls loose from her quickly and turns away. Anything unexpected embarrasses him.

She stands in front of the house and waves. He can see her in his rearview mirror. He sticks his arm out of the window and waves back at her without turning his head.

7 8   Jürgen comes back from his vacation three days late. It was completely different this time. In the past, he had always gone on tours or to resorts where he had booked ahead.

Before he goes home, he drinks one last beer in the Gasthaus zur Mitte.

Muckel, Penzing's daughter-in-law, serves him. Her husband, Lothar, is sitting in his butcher's apron at the regulars' table and holding forth.

Jürgen is reminded of a girl he has not thought about for a long time. Heidrun.

Muckel has her arms folded in front of her on the bar. Her breasts rest on her arms as if they wanted to look out the window.

Did you have any adventures?

Jürgen answers with a shrug of resignation: Nothing worth mentioning.

He's annoyed with himself for lying.

I really had quite a good time, he adds.

You should find yourself a girl friend and travel together, Muckel says. Then it'll be more fun.

What would have been the point of telling her anything? Jürgen says now.

It's always the same old story. There's nobody you can really talk to.

He sits at Penzing's bar for a while, uncertain about what he should do.

He starts thinking up excuses for coming back so late but then stops himself. Who do I have to apologize to? he says. The firm maybe, but that's it.

Everything is just the same at home. Adolf is sitting half asleep in his armchair next to the telephone, the way he has for as long as Jürgen can remember. His mouth, his cheeks, and his temples are sunken in. He seems even thinner and frailer than he was before.

Edith sits opposite him on the sofa and knits.

The room looks somehow different. Jürgen gradually becomes aware of small changes that Adolf never would have permitted before.

Edith greets him warmly. Adolf mumbles something under his breath. Then Edith gets Jürgen something to eat.

She didn't look like Adolf's wife anymore, Jürgen thinks. But she still looked like my mother. I thought she looked better than the way she used to.

But she almost seemed to be a stranger in our apartment, maybe a sister of my father's or an acquaintance who was keeping house for him.

By removing Edith from the family in this way, Jürgen is unconsciously trying to separate himself from his own past.

His dream of a new life with Giovanna comes to an end the next morning.

He drives his car to work, but the strain on him is even greater than if he had taken the trolley. He stalls twice when the light turns green. The horns blowing behind him drive him wild.

Once, he gets into the wrong lane. He slows down and signals, but the drivers in the next lane make no move to let him in. He finally stops. The honking behind him begins instantly.

That wouldn't have happened in Sassari or Rome. Everybody there drives the way he pleases, and the others let him. Since this is so, everyone can drive any way he likes.

He begins to sense that freedom can only be achieved collectively, but he is unable to articulate this insight clearly. Individual freedom contains an element of terrorism if it goes beyond the degree of freedom that everyone else enjoys.

Jürgen feels that the difference between Germans and Italians is evident in the difference between the two styles of driving.

In the locker room, Jürgen has to put up with the usual ribbing that anyone who has been missing for a few days has to expect.

It's understandable that the absentee's co-workers feel entitled to a little revenge. A capitalist doesn't hire any new help if someone is missing, and that means everyone else just has to work that much harder. The work has to be done, but the pay remains the same.

Somebody asks: Did you have a little accident?

He sticks his thumb between his middle and index fingers and wiggles his hips around.

Somebody else says: Maybe he got stuck somewhere.

He puts his hand between his legs and pretends he can't pull it out again.

7 9   After the morning break, Jürgen is summoned to the personnel office.

Uncle Hans is seated at the desk of the personnel manager.

Franse, the personnel manager, is standing next to him.
Uncle Hans is in charge.

He mentions Jürgen's late return from vacation only in passing. The firm can tolerate that, even though it is sufficient grounds for dismissal without notice.

His attitude with Jürgen is paternalistic. He inquires after Adolf. Did you have a nice vacation?

Then he gets down to business.

The situation is this, Jürgen, Mehlig says, addressing him with the formal "*Sie.*" Jürgen can't remember Mehlig ever addressing him that way before.

Mehlig was turning to him as an old friend of the family. For several weeks now, leaflets agitating against the firm's management had been circulating in the plant.

Let me have one of them, Franse.

Personnel Manager Franse is an important personage in N. Local committee chairman for the CDU. Rumor has it that Mehlig himself was responsible for getting Franse that post.

Together with Bach Hein—and with Adolf, too, before Adolf's illness—Franse is one of the regulars who meet at Penzing's every Sunday morning. They are in the hiking club together, too. Franse's nickname is Godfather Franse.

Hi there, Godfather, people in these parts say when they meet an old acquaintance.

Godfather Franse hands Uncle Hans a leaflet, which he in turn passes on to Jürgen. Jürgen hardly dares glance at it for fear Mehlig will think he is interested in what the leaflet says. Go ahead and read it, Mehlig says.

Jürgen reads something about a threatened shutdown of the plant.

I want to know who's putting these leaflets out, Mehlig says in a friendly tone. And I'd appreciate it if you could help me find out. Mehlig's request is embarrassing for Jürgen. He has a pretty good idea who is distributing the leaflets in the plant: Freddy.

. . .

He tries to talk himself out of this jam. He spends his whole day at the plate shears. He doesn't have much contact with anyone.

Uncle Hans hints that Jürgen could be transferred to a job that wouldn't tie him down to one spot so much, a job that would let him get around more in the plant.

Jürgen claims he is perfectly satisfied with the job he has now. Mehlig's offer appeals to him, but Freddy would find out right away that Jürgen had betrayed him.

It's left that for the time being Jürgen will just keep his eyes and ears open in the section he's in now.

8 0   The rumors about the firm possibly closing down evoke varied reactions among the workers. Bach Hein and his group and the Social Democratic majority in the workers' council call the leaflet campaign irresponsible. All it does is stir up the workers and undermine the authority of the workers' council.

The dissidents, with Freddy as their spokesman, argue that the leaflets are not attacking the council or its chairman. They are directed instead at the firm's management, and they urge the management to make a binding public statement that it does not intend to shut the plant down. All the workers' council is asked to do is convince management to make such a statement.

Bach Hein's group replies that no one can expect the firm's management to make an official statement on every rumor that comes along. It has to be left to the chairman of the workers' council to decide for himself whether he will raise this issue at one of his regular meetings with the plant's management.

He, Bach Hein, is not going to let anybody tell him what he should or shouldn't do, especially not any council members who ran on a ticket inimical to the union.

Furthermore, there is no need to bring the subject up.

He is convinced that the firm will inform the workers' council about any major decisions it has under consideration.

Dreamer, Freddy calls out.

That's enough from you, Niebling, Bach Hein snaps back. I helped build Fahlbusch & Siebert up again with my own hands. Do you think I'd sit around twiddling my thumbs if this plant was about to be closed down? I've been in union politics since before you were born.

Yeah, and you sold the unions out to the SPD and the capitalists in exchange for a few lousy political appointments, Freddy retorts.

You rotten little bastard! Bach Hein shouts. He's on the verge of a stroke.

That's slander. That's grounds for immediate dismissal. I'll have your ass in court.

Most of the workers feel helpless and confused.

The fear of losing their jobs only muddles their thinking all the more.

Some of them strike out at the leaflet campaign. Spreading rumors like that just gives the directors ideas. If they hear enough of that stuff, they really will shut the plant down.

In the discussions the workers have on the job, in their breaks, and in the bars, they give vent to a shapeless anarchism which, lacking organization and a point of view, can be expressed only as blind rage, rage over prevailing injustice, the unfair distribution of goods and wealth, the workers' total subjugation to the men at the top.

Most of them identify with the three major political parties only briefly and on certain occasions; that is, when there is an election. They all have enough class consciousness to realize that no significant improvements will be made for the working class no matter which of those parties is in power.

.   .   .

It doesn't matter who's holding the reins, the men say. It's always us working slobs who wind up pulling the wagon.

The rival splinter groups that stand to the left of the SPD are of no interest to the workingman, even though there may be occasional reports about them on television or in the papers. The workers are indifferent to what these small political groups consider the most burning of issues: the civil rights struggle in the Soviet Union, the Prague intellectuals, the situation of opposition writers in the German Democratic Republic.

A man whose real income is constantly shrinking, whose very existence is threatened by the rising cost of living, and who has to worry about losing his job, a man who sees the demand made on him in the factory increasing constantly while the rights of the citizen are being steadily eroded away, a man like that is not interested in knowing that Bukowski is holding a press conference in Zurich today and will be received in the White House tomorrow. A worker who is banned from the factory and deprived of the only means he has to earn a living will not receive a grant from the City of Hamburg.

Most of the workers know about a certain party. Many of them know in their hearts that it could represent a real alternative to the parties in control in Bonn, parties whose members in the Bundestag do nothing but raise their own standard of living by voting increases in per-diem allowances. Every worker has some idea about this party, knows what its goals are. Some workers know that this party is right, but almost all of them are afraid of it, too. The German Communist Party.

But it's not the party's position that they fear.

They fear their own circles, their friends, relatives, neighbors. They fear losing the respect of their communities; they fear slander, the loss of their jobs, surveillance by the political police and other agencies commissioned with defending the constitution, all the things they would be exposed to if they threw their lot in with the party.

. . .

This is the fear that divides us, muddles our thinking, and triggers our personal crises.

We live on this fear, reap the rewards of it, and die of it.

8 1 Jürgen joins Freddy's faction.

When Giovanna comes, he'll introduce Freddy to her.

He'll tell her about their struggle at the plant.

She'll see that he's on her side.

Uncle Hans summons him again.

I want to make things clear to you, Jürgen. It's your job to identify the troublemakers, not join forces with them.

Jürgen plays the confident tactician who has the situation well under control: I thought it would be best to join the most radical group in the plant if I wanted to find out who has been distributing the leaflets and spreading these rumors.

Mehlig claims that he realized even then that no good could come of this.

It is obvious in talking to Mehlig that he still places all the blame on Freddy. We all know the kind of impression someone like that can make on a politically naïve youngster, he says. As far as I'm concerned, it was Niebling who got your boy Jürgen into this mess.

Mehlig has retired and is said to have negotiated himself a six-figure pension. He's one of the few people at Fahlbusch & Siebert who are better off after the closing down of the plant than they were before.

His living room commands a view of the whole river valley.

Down in the valley, the riverbank marks the town limits of N. After looking for a while, I spot the factory buildings. It's impossible to overlook the one large warehouse with its roof blown off. Mehlig follows my gaze.

.   .   .

Yes, he says. Jürgen could have spared himself all that trouble. There were plans in the works to have those buildings torn down anyhow. The office building is the only one that will be turned to some other use.

The rumors and leaflets continue to circulate in the plant week after week. Every new rumor only seems to confirm the workers' feeling that they are being sold out. The longer the workers' council and the firm's management keep their silence, the greater the workers' rage and feeling of helplessness.

Toward the end of October, a new rumor—again disseminated in leaflets—begins to circulate in the plant. The claim is that Fahlbusch & Siebert had already been bought up back in the spring by a huge concern working in the same line. And a year before that, the concern that now owns Fahlbusch & Siebert had sold the controlling interest in its stock to a North American firm.

The only reason Fahlbusch & Siebert had been bought out was to close it down as soon as possible and get rid of it as a competitor.

Now discussions in the plant take on a clearly anti-American character. The workers rail against the American monopoly capitalism that is destroying small and medium-sized manufacturers in Europe.

The inadequate organization of the workers—and particularly the lack of a genuine anti-monopolistic organization—prevents them from seeing the impending closure of Fahlbusch & Siebert in terms of the historical concept applicable to it, that of imperialism.

The fear of losing their jobs keeps most of the workers from pushing their demands for clarification of the questions that are plaguing them all and from fighting to keep the plant open, possibly even assuming control of it themselves if necessary. The fear of losing their jobs prevents them from taking up the fight to save their jobs.

This fear has sources other than economic ones. The ideology dominant in our society has managed to convince us that it is an individual's own fault if he has no job. If he is out of work, he has no one but himself to blame. The capitalistic economic system is certainly not to blame.

The result is that a man out of work has to face a major personal crisis without getting any support whatsoever from the norms of his society. Only if his house burns down or if his wife dies does he suffer a comparably disastrous blow; but with the help of his own experience of life, his insurance, and the sympathy of his friends, he'll be able to handle those crises much better than he can a period of unemployment.

Men out of work drive their cars into town in the morning and just hang around so that their neighbors, and sometimes even their wives, won't suspect that they've been laid off. If an unemployed man gets caught at home, he'll claim he's sick. Or he offers some other excuse: he's working a short shift; he's being trained for a different job; he's been promoted and has to take some further schooling; he's quit his job and is just waiting until he starts work on a new and better one.

For older men, the crisis may lead to problems with their wives and children, to depression, even suicide.

Younger people who go through a long period of unemployment but do not suffer serious material deprivation at the same time are given to crime, violence, and emotional outbursts. Crimes against the public weal are fairly common.

In terms of political thought, this phenomenon represents a glaring inconsistency.

A system that professes to be humane and criticizes other systems for being inhumane lets human beings degenerate. A system that is constantly insisting that other countries uphold basic human rights is itself incapable of realizing the most important of those rights—the right to work.

8 2   Giovanna comes to Germany at the end of October, 1974. When she wakes up at dawn, her train is passing through the lowlands of the Upper Rhine somewhere between Baden-Baden and Frankfurt am Main. The first station sign she sees says Karlsruhe.

It is a gray day, cold, damp, overcast. The sun had been shining in Rome the afternoon before. People were sitting outside in front of cafés and restaurants. It was dazzlingly clear and pleasantly warm, not intolerably hot the way it is in August and September. Fall is a lovely season in Rome, almost as beautiful as March and April.

A heavy pall seems to hang over Germany. She imagines that a plane could fly over this country and the passengers wouldn't be able to see it at all under this thick gray cover. For Italian Germanophiles, the semidarkness of this country harbors romantic mysteries. Its damp landscape is peopled by water gods and gorgeous nixies rarely seen by humans.

The German past is bathed in a warm glow cast by the thoughts and ideas of German philosophers who needed their country's broken light in order to pursue unbroken trains of thought. Germany's brooks and rivers are the vital arteries from which the country draws strength, fertility, and intellectual vigor. Tacitus was among the first to feel the magical appeal of the Rhine.

All Giovanna sees as her train flies past stations or stops at them is grayish human masses waiting for the commuter train that will take them to work. She can smell the dank mustiness in the clothes of the people who board the train to ride for another station or two.

She has to change trains in Mannheim.

On the platform, she is carried along by a shoving, pushing, hurrying crowd of people. Their faces are pale, unfriendly, unsmiling. No one takes notice of anyone else. It's rare to see two people talking to each other. Nobody just strolls along. The mob silently sweeps up everyone in its path.

She can't find a bar or café anywhere in the station where she can have a cup of coffee.

She finally ends up in the station restaurant and stands at the serving counter. Without saying anything, the woman working behind the counter motions to her to sit at a table.

Giovanna doesn't understand and orders a coffee.

I told you to sit down, the woman says.

Somewhat startled, Giovanna takes a seat.

After a while two waiters appear. They are speaking Italian. One of them moves away. The other turns to her.

She resists the temptation to address him in Italian and gives her order in German.

Late that morning she arrives in K.

She exchanges her money at the station and is surprised to see how few marks she gets for her lire.

In the trolley, she calculates that a streetcar ticket costs exactly seven times as much here as it does in Rome. If the Germans have to pay such high prices at home, she thinks, they have to buy cheaply abroad to get by. Seen in this light, the exchange rate is understandable.

The front door at the Schütrumpfs' apartment house is stuck. Giovanna shoves and yanks at it in vain when the buzzer sounds. Adolf finally shuffles to the door.

His face lights up when he sees her. He strikes her as a bit senile. He greets her warmly but doesn't know who she is or what her name is. He tries to take her suitcase but can't manage it. Until then, Giovanna hasn't realized how weak he really is.

They sit together in the living room. Adolf is drinking schnapps and beer. Giovanna is having a liqueur.

Adolf is trying to give her a rough idea of the major events of his life.

He has traveled extensively, has met the most important figures of his time, and was an eyewitness to the most significant historical events of the century.

He speaks at length about World War I and the German Revolution of 1918.

Giovanna understands little of what he is saying because he jumps about in time and strings disparate historical periods together without making any transitions between them. He keeps losing the thread of his narrative; then, after a brief lapse into distracted silence, he picks it up again at some unrelated point.

Much of what he says is no more than unintelligible muttering. He often fades off into conversations with himself, as if he were relating his story for his own benefit.

His tone turns aggressive. He works himself up into a rage over certain people and events.

Toward evening, Edith comes home. She, too, extends Giovanna a warm greeting. Our Jürgen always did have good taste, she jokes.

My husband and I are very open-minded. An Italian is just as welcome here as a Frenchman. We find we don't have so much in common with Orientals, of course.

Then Jürgen comes home from work.

Well, this is where I live. Do you like it?

She nods.

She feels cramped. The apartment is too warm, and stuffed full of furniture. There's hardly any room to move around in. The air is bad and oppressive. The odor Adolf gives off makes it even worse.

The windows can't be opened because the windowsills are so jammed with plants.

Jürgen goes into the kitchen to get something to eat. In the meantime, Adolf tells Giovanna where all the many souvenirs on the walls and in the china cabinet come from.

While Giovanna is in the bathroom, Edith asks: Does Giovanna always dress like that? I mean she should make more of what she has.

Such an attractive girl, and then she goes and dresses so that you can't see anything of her.

After Adolf has gone to sleep in his armchair, Jürgen suggests they go to Penzing's for a beer. Giovanna agrees out of curiosity.

She is struck by the fact that Jürgen is showing her off like an important new acquisition.

Of course I was proud as a peacock, he says. None of the guys I know around here have ever had a girl like her.

Giovanna feels as if she is in Sardinia. She is the only woman in the bar.

They sit at a table in a corner.

Old man Penzing himself comes over to wait on them and be introduced to Giovanna. What? You came all the way up here from Italy just to see this Kassel hustler?

And he winks at them.

What's a hustler? Giovanna asks.

Sort of a go-getter.

And what's a go-getter?

Well, somebody who goes right after what he wants.

Giovanna has a lot of trouble understanding the older local people. The idiom of K. is typical for an urban lower-middle-class and proletarian population.

Here, hold my sandwich while I punch you in the nose.

8 3 Giovanna spends her first few days wandering aimlessly around in N. and on into K.

The Schütrumpfs have fixed up the sofa in the living room for her to sleep on. Jürgen and Edith are away at work during the day. Adolf spends most of his time sitting in his armchair, dozing or staring into space.

. . .

In the evening, Jürgen takes her to Penzing's or to a movie, some-times to a restaurant in K. Don't you have any friends we can visit? Giovanna asks. She wants to talk to people.

K. seems strange to her.

Most Italian cities still retain their historical centers. The build-ings follow the contours of the old streets, and the old façades are preserved even if there are new buildings behind them.

Potemkin villages.

Giovanna finds the unrelieved functionality and ugliness of down-town K. staggering. Streets several lanes wide carve up the residential and business sections, isolating one part of town from another. The cars drive as if they were on the autobahn, not in a city. There is nothing to see on these streets.

The business streets downtown add up to nothing more than a big marketplace whose sole function is to move goods as quickly as possible. Large sections of the downtown area do not seem to be inhabited.

She is astonished to see how thousands of people pour out of the buildings when the workday is over and leave the downtown streets deserted within an hour.

Everything seems to have its function. Nothing is there for the sake of beauty. The city looks as if it hadn't existed thirty years ago. The few older buildings that are left look as if a madman had plunked them down randomly. It is impossible to imagine what this city might have looked like in earlier times.

Giovanna soon realizes that Adolf and Edith don't approve of her spending whole days just walking around.

Adolf suggests that she go for walks through the riverside park with him on nice days.

She goes with him a few times, but she wants to learn more than the muddled tales of a sick old man can tell her. Edith invites her to go out with her, too. Giovanna joins her for an afternoon in the Café Reuter with Frau Sangmeister and Fräulein Wettlaufer.

Jürgen does his best to please her. In the evenings, he drags her along on a tour of all the downtown bars where he thinks there might be some people of interest to her. And some of these people do in fact look promising. They're the right types, at least as far as you can tell from their clothes and general appearance. But the expedition is a flop anyhow.

They run into the same thing everywhere. People stand crowded together at the bars; the tables are all taken; everyone is drinking excessively; the noise in the room creates the impression that a lively discussion is in progress. But in reality people are talking in small isolated groups of twos and threes. A larger group is a rarity. Communication is limited to private circles.

Worst of all, Jürgen doesn't know anyone anywhere. It doesn't take Giovanna long to see that Jürgen won't be of any help to her in getting to know people or in learning more about life in Germany. She doesn't hold this against him.

She quickly understands that this society, which is the major producer of wealth in Western Europe, is made up of people who don't talk with each other, who adopt ready-made opinions from the mass media as their own, and who cut themselves off from each other. The form of community that is most efficient for the production of goods calls for the total isolation of the individual. For all practical purposes, the nuclear family is the largest social organization there is.

This is an anthill in which people display the discipline and diligence of creatures guided by remote control.

Giovanna tells Jürgen what her impressions are.

He is unmoved by this and assumes an air of superiority.

He has been aware of all that for a long time.

Culturally the Federal Republic is dead as a doornail.

Giovanna wonders if she might not be mistaken.

She does not want to give herself up to resignation so soon.

If workers did not give in to resignation, capital could not exploit them. It's resignation that makes a housewife keep on doing her chores, raising her children, and teaching them resignation.

Giovanna makes the best of things by spending hours in the county library reading German newspapers and poring over whatever books catch her eye. A few people speak to her.

She decides to ignore the fact that Edith and Adolf obviously regard her as Jürgen's future wife, that he seems to harbor hopes that she will marry him, and that she still hasn't found anyone with whom she can really talk.

She decides to look for a job, rent a room, and go her own way.

8 4   On a Sunday after Giovanna has been in the Federal Republic barely ten days, she persuades Jürgen to go to see the Pittuis with her. Jürgen has gotten their address from Francesco. They live on Mönchebergstrasse in K.

Jürgen is embarrassed by the condition of the building. The outside walls are in need of repair. Several windows are cracked. The lock on the front door is broken. The owner has not been willing to invest in new garbage cans. The courtyard is filthy. The stairwell was apparently not renovated after the war. Everyone knows about these buildings that West German speculators rent out to foreign workers at exorbitant rates.

In the entranceway Jürgen makes another embarrassing discovery. A battered sign names the owner and the owner's local representative.

The house belongs to Edith's brother Bübi, the doctor; and Jürgen's father is his representative.

Giovanna notices Jürgen's surprise over the sign, and she looks at it, too.

As they go up the stairs, Jürgen tries to explain to her that Adolf is helpless to do anything if his uncle is not willing to fix up the building.

Giovanna's Sardinian sense of family honor makes it hard for her to accept Jürgen's excuses. The uncle is part of the family, too. Every member of a family is responsible for the delinquencies of the others.

Do you expect me to go to Uncle Bübi and tell him to keep his buildings in good condition just because you have friends living here?

That's just what I expect, Giovanna replies.

The Pittuis have three rooms, kitchen, hallway, and bath. Patricio, whose wife and children are living in Orgosolo, has one room to himself. One room serves Francesco and his wife, Franca, as a living room and bedroom. Their three children—Massimo, nine; Letitia, seven; and Lavinia, four—share the third room.

The apartment is in as poor shape as the rest of the house. The Pittuis complain that the landlord won't fix anything. The wiring, which is installed over the plaster, is not firmly attached to the walls, and a few junction boxes and outlets are coming loose. The whole electrical system is criminally substandard. The chimneys are clogged and don't draw properly. The sewage pipes are corroded and leaky. The house smells of garbage. The plumbing fixtures are ancient and run-down. Nothing has been done to spruce the place up for decades.

The Pittuis are angry. The rent is too high, 380 marks a month, plus utilities. Now the landlord is demanding 100 marks more for subletting to Patricio. They are refusing to pay.

Jürgen is grateful to Giovanna for not mentioning who the landlord's local agent is.

The Pittuis serve red wine, olives, and some cheese that a friend has brought from Sardinia.

They often get together with other Sardinians in the area. There are over a hundred Sardinians living in K. alone.

Everyone defers to Francesco's wife, Franca. She sits in an armchair at the head of the table and knits. The two men and the children set the table.

She contributes little to the conversation, but it is clear that she is the head of the family.

She speaks German haltingly, as do the two men.

This is the first time Jürgen has ever been in a foreign worker's apartment.

Everything looks different from what he had expected. He'd had no idea of how it would look. But if he'd had an idea, it wouldn't have been like this at all.

Francesco Pittui has been working at Fahlbusch & Siebert for nine years. His family joined him five years ago. They have been living in this apartment on Mönchebergstrasse ever since. Patricio came to Germany a year ago. He knows Giovanna because she always stayed at his house during her vacations in Sardinia. Giovanna and Francesco's family scarcely know each other.

They talk about the hardships of emigration.

The Italian constitution explicitly guarantees the right to work as a basic human right.

The Pittui brothers regard the incapacity of their government and of the economy to provide work for all Italians as a violation of the constitution.

What kind of country and what kind of a ruling class is it that forces millions of people to emigrate? they ask.

Giovanna asks them what life is like for foreign workers.

Finding a place to live is the worst problem. Most Germans won't rent to foreigners. They are at the mercy of speculators. A lot of foreign workers who don't come from Common Market countries don't have work permits. They have to take any job they can get; they're cheated out of part of their wages; and they're not covered by any insurance.

But even the workers who have come into the country legally are usually not given jobs commensurate with their abilities and are paid less than German workers.

Massimo and Letitia are having trouble at school. There aren't enough classes and teachers for the foreign children.

We're brought here to increase the Germans' wealth, but they treat us like slaves, Patricio says.

Both brothers are members of the Communist Party, but they have not sought out any contact with German comrades for fear of losing their jobs. It's not a good idea to be a Communist if you work at Fahlbusch & Siebert, they say.

Jürgen has seen them at the plant only in their work clothes. Now, when they're at home on a Sunday afternoon, they're wearing old-fashioned black suits and dark ties. They strike him as conservative and of another time, like the farmers and artisans in family photographs from before World War I.

Their whole bearing is strange and solemn.

In keeping with the day of rest.

After the first bottle of wine, conversation picks up. The two men tell stories. Everyone laughs. They're speaking Sardinian now. Jürgen can't understand a word. Sometimes Giovanna quickly tells him the gist of a story. Jürgen feels free and at ease.

Toward evening the men begin cooking.

They make spaghetti, fry some lamb chops, and prepare a salad.

Jürgen asks if all Sardinian men do the cooking.

Giovanna laughs softly and turns to Franca, who is sitting placidly in her chair.

Franca smiles as Giovanna answers the question.

It's a matter of habit, Giovanna says. As shepherds, they have to learn to take care of themselves when they spend months at a time in the mountains. They think it's fun to pretend they're still out in the fields alone with their flocks, particularly when they're here in Germany. You see?

After supper they start singing.

The Pittuis ask Giovanna to describe her trip to Germany and her experiences so far.

She skillfully takes on the role of the soloist while Patricio and Francesco play the chorus.

Jürgen feels as if he were on the moon.

Giovanna is depressed later that evening when they are sitting in the Schütrumpfs' living room. She's dying to go to bed, but there's still a detective film on the TV. Edith is watching listlessly. Adolf's head keeps falling onto his chest. Jürgen stays up to keep Giovanna company.

Giovanna would sleep in the hallway at the Pittuis' if she could.

Jürgen is wondering if he shouldn't suggest that they rent a little apartment together somewhere.

Not with just one bedroom and one living room.

There'd have to be a bedroom for each of them. Maybe that way she'd be willing to do it.

He decides to propose this to her at an opportune moment.

Don't worry about the money. I'm making decent wages. I can take care of the food and all that. That would be the way to do it.

Step by step, they'll become a regular married couple.

8 5   From now on, Giovanna goes to see Franca almost every day. She helps her with her shopping and housework and gives the children German lessons.

Franca has two jobs as a cleaning woman. At five in the morning, before she goes to her first job, she gets breakfast ready for the family. The older children go to school alone, and Lavinia stays home. Franca is back in the apartment at about eight-thirty. She goes to her second job in the afternoon just before the men come home from work. They make their supper themselves.

Through the Pittuis, Giovanna gets to know other Sardinian families.

Jürgen complains a bit.

I thought you wanted to see Germany.

Good, let's go, Giovanna says. Show it to me.

The next Sunday, Jürgen takes her to see Uncle Erich and Aunt Hilde in their village. She likes that.

But even here she has the feeling that it's harder to get to know people and to talk to them in Germany.

Giovanna meets Freddy Niebling at the Pittuis' too.

The men bring him home from work with them. Freddy is a friend of the family's.

The men talk politics.

When they realize that Giovanna is interested, they tell her about the plant, too.

Jürgen hears about this during a morning break. Freddy says something complimentary about Jürgen's friend from Sardinia. Jürgen is annoyed. He doesn't like the idea of Freddy and Giovanna meeting if he isn't with them.

Freddy is unaware of Jürgen's concern.

He is one of those men who think a woman has to decide for herself with whom she spends her time and what she does. Jürgen has no desire to be a patriarch like Adolf, but he thinks a man has to take some care with a woman to see that she doesn't run off on him. It's particularly important not to leave her alone too much if she doesn't have anything to do.

Jürgen feels some sympathy for the men who force two or three children on their wives, make them do all the housework alone, and send them out to work half days as well. That keeps a woman from getting any funny ideas. It worries Jürgen that Giovanna is so independent and has so much time at her disposal.

8 6   Freddy has other things on his mind.

He urges Jürgen to make the most of his ties to Mehlig.

How do you picture that?

You just say you'd like to know where you're at. Whether you've got a steady job or not. I thought he was a friend of your family's.

Jürgen doesn't like the idea. You don't pick the brains of an old family friend.

Freddy puts pressure on him: We're talking about the fate of six hundred workers here.

If it's true that the firm has been sold, then Mehlig is a bastard. If that's the way it really is, then he should have told the workers' council, especially if the plant is going to be closed down.

Konrad suggests another possibility: Maybe Bach Hein has known all along and just hasn't told you anything.

It's Bach Hein's duty to keep the entire workers' council informed, Freddy replies.

Then he turns back to Jürgen: Make up your mind, Jürgen. What's more important? Six hundred jobs or a family friendship?

When Jürgen agrees to speak to Mehlig, he doesn't do it because of his six hundred fellow workers at Fahlbusch & Siebert or to please Freddy.

He's afraid of only one thing: Freddy might tell Giovanna that he refused to speak with Mehlig. After the morning break, he tells Bach Hein that he has to go see Director Mehlig.

Bach Hein telephones the office.

Schütrumpf should be sent over.

What do they want with you? Bach Hein asks suspiciously.

Oh, nothing. Maybe they want me to do some installation work somewhere.

Bach Hein nods knowingly. Connections. He knows that old man Schütrumpf and Mehlig are friends. N. is still a village. To look at it, you might think N. had been absorbed by K. long ago. Anyone who doesn't know the city's history might think N. has always been a part of K. proper.

But if you know N. from the inside, you know that much of the old communications network is still intact. Old-time residents pass around a lot of gossip and rumors.

And what will become of your little girl friend if you go away on a job?

What do you mean?

That Italian girl.

So Bach Hein knows about that, too.

Do you think she'll want to sit here all alone in K.?

Jürgen's plan is simple.

Mehlig will have to come clean with him and promise to find him a job somewhere else if the plant is shut down. Unless Mehlig is willing to guarantee this, Jürgen won't give him any information.

Well, what do you know? Mehlig says. Little Jürgen is just like his old man. Your father has always had a streak of healthy skepticism.

All right. Since it's you, I promise.

I've known you ever since you were knee high to a grasshopper.

Did you know I was even at your christening?

All of a sudden, Mehlig has reverted to the familiar "*du*" with Jürgen again.

I swear to you on a stack of Bibles that you'll get a job somewhere else if we close down.

Does that satisfy you?

Jürgen tries to dig a little deeper: Can you tell me approximately when that might be?

Uncle Hans draws the line there: Sorry, Jürgen. I can't tell you anything more. But in any case, you're assured of a job.

Now tell me what you've found out.

.　　.　　.

Jürgen has already prepared an answer to this question. He has some leads, but it's too early to name any names yet. He doesn't want to speak too soon and maybe accuse someone unjustly. He'll be meeting the person he suspects in the next few days after work. He may have to offer to help the suspect produce the leaflets.

Freddy asks at lunchtime what Mehlig said.

Jürgen is leery about saying anything. He can't know how Freddy will use the information he gives him. Jürgen wouldn't put it past Freddy to stir up the whole work force.

The firm's management would immediately suspect Jürgen of being behind all the turmoil. He is the only one who knows that the plant is going to be closed. What else could Uncle Hans mean by his promise that he would find Jürgen another job?

Jürgen distorts Mehlig's statement a bit.

He didn't say anything. For all practical purposes, nothing at all. He said we needn't worry about our jobs.

That'll be the day, Konrad growls.

Couldn't you get a bit more than that out of him? Freddy asks.

What do you want me to do? Put thumbscrews on him?

That's what he deserves, the lousy shit, Freddy says. We ought to burn the place down around his ears.

Bach Hein is suddenly there.

That big mouth of yours is going to get you into an awful lot of trouble someday, Niebling.

8 7   On Friday, November 15, 1974, Adolf Schütrumpf illegally evicts the Pittui family from their apartment. In a fit of senile rage that momentarily overcomes the lethargy of his sclerotic brain, he arranges to have a locksmith and a moving van with four men meet him at the Mönchebergstrasse building.

.   .   .

Oddly enough, it is Giovanna who precipitates this action.

At breakfast, she tells Adolf about her Sardinian friends. Adolf pricks up his ears: Pittui?

But he doesn't betray any sign of interest. It's that Pittui family that has refused to pay a hundred marks more a month for subletting. They've been a thorn in Adolf's side for a long time.

With his old man's cunning, Adolf pretends that he is negotiating with the owner of the building to make some urgently needed repairs. The condition of those buildings is a scandal.

Giovanna falls into his trap. She readily answers his questions about the family's habits and way of life, telling him among other things that the men leave the house at six-thirty and that Signora Pittui is out cleaning until eight-thirty in the morning.

Two days later, when the men leave for work, Adolf and his crew are ready for action.

To be on the safe side, he knocks on the apartment door, making sure that Signora Pittui is not there.

The children haven't left for school yet. Suspecting nothing, they open the door.

Adolf sends the locksmith home.

Then he tells the movers to get to work.

The children watch in stunned amazement as the men quickly clear the apartment.

After a while, little Massimo tries to sneak out.

He doesn't know anyone in this building, but there's an Italian family the Pittuis know living just a few blocks away.

He wants to get help.

Adolf sits in the kitchen with the children and tries to press candy on them.

Where are you going? he asks in a friendly tone.

To the bathroom, Massimo says softly.

Wait, I'll go with you.

Adolf stands guard at the apartment door while the boy goes to the bathroom. He doesn't know what he should do with the children when the movers are done.

Shortly after eight, Giovanna arrives to make coffee for Franca and to look after Lavinia. On the stairs, she encounters the moving men carrying the furniture down.

The apartment door is open. The apartment is nearly empty.

Outraged, she turns to Adolf.

He crumples visibly when he sees Giovanna, but he stubbornly defends his action anyhow, claiming that the Pittuis have already cheated his brother-in-law out of 1,200 marks.

What are you going to do with the furniture?

He'll have it stored away as security for the sum the Pittuis owe.

He sticks by his decision to take the furniture to the mover's warehouse. As Giovanna continues to object, he puts her off with a weary gesture. You haven't the faintest idea of what this is all about.

Just keep out of it. It's nothing for women to trouble their heads over.

Giovanna and Franca are standing at the gate at Fahlbusch & Siebert when the morning break begins.

They ask to see the Pittui brothers and Jürgen.

Jürgen promises to speak with his father after work. This business is embarrassing to him.

Giovanna insists that he come right away. Where will the Pittuis sleep tonight?

Jürgen is in a bind.

He knows that Adolf will not change his mind. But Giovanna won't let him off the hook. He has no business defending his father. It's his duty to put on all the pressure he can. If necessary, he should threaten to move out.

She will not spend another night under the same roof with this monster.

.   .   .

Francesco and Patricio see little point in this whole discussion. What Jürgen does is of no interest to them.

They will simply go to the warehouse, ask for their furniture, and move back in.

Adolf will have to pay the movers. The Pittuis have rented the apartment, and they have a right to live in it.

Jürgen is pleased with this solution. It leaves the initiative with the family directly concerned. He is even willing to call Adolf and find out where the furniture was taken.

Adolf is suspicious. Why do you want to know? Jürgen has a ready answer. That's another thing he has inherited from Edith. She considers ready answers and good excuses the most important things you can have in life. A favorite saying of hers is: My grandmother got a licking once because she didn't have a good excuse.

One of the Pittui brothers has to have some papers that are in a box.
All right, Adolf says.
The furniture is stored at Bröckelmannsen & Grund's warehouse.
He meant to say "Bröckelmann sen. & Grund."

8 8   By lunchtime, Patricio and Francesco Pittui are back at the plant.

The warehouse foreman won't let them have their furniture. Giovanna has rented two rooms for them in a pension for the night.

The Sardinians turn to Freddy for help. The first thing Freddy does is send Jürgen out of earshot.

It's your father we're talking about.
You must be able to understand why we don't want you here.

Jürgen complains.
You go sit somewhere else if you don't like having me around. Do you think I'm going to tell my old man everything you say?

.   .   .

Jürgen finally gives in.
   Okay. I'll go.

Freddy tells the Pittuis that they and the family can stay with him.
His parents moved to Düsseldorf some time ago. Patricio can sleep in
the attic. Francesco and Franca can have his parents' bedroom, and
the children can sleep in the living room. All he needs is his own
room. It's Friday, and they won't be able to initiate any legal action
until after the weekend anyhow.

When Jürgen comes home, Edith hands him a note.
   Adolf is stubbornly self-righteous when Jürgen reproaches him for
what he has done. Better to make a quick and painful end of a bad
show than have it drag on forever. If Giovanna has left because of a
trifling business like this, then he's better off without her. Adolf has
been married to Edith for twenty-five years. He's not about to let
anybody tell him how to manage his affairs now. If you don't pay,
you get out. It's that simple.

Jürgen holds Giovanna's note in his hand as if it were a sacred relic.
Dear Jürgen, you can reach me at the Pension Westend. Forgive me,
and thanks for everything you and your parents have done for me.
Despite what has happened now. Affectionately, Giovanna.

His mind goes blank for several minutes.
   Giovanna is gone.
   When he comes out of his fog, his thoughts are still confused.
Then, in a matter of seconds, he is possessed by an idea that sends
him running out of the house.

He has to speak with her right away. Explain everything to her. He
loves her. She has to stay with him. He can't live without her. He'll
rent an apartment now. If she likes, an apartment large enough for
the Pittuis to live with them, too. You are the woman I've waited for
all my life. A real human being at last.

.   .   .

As he is driving to the Pension Westend, his imagination starts working overtime.

Giovanna is already regretting her decision and is on her way to the Schütrumpfs'. At the trolley stop on S. Square, he sees a girl who looks like Giovanna standing in the crowd.

He looks for a parking place, can't find one, leaves his car in the middle of the street, and runs to the trolley stop. The last passengers are getting onto the streetcar headed for N. Giovanna isn't standing there anymore.

Without thinking, he gets on the trolley and pushes his way through the dense crowd of standing passengers. By the time he reaches the front of the car, he is drenched with sweat and filled with hatred for the people in the streetcar. Can't they understand how important it is for him to move through quickly?

He gets off at City Hall and sinks exhausted onto a bench. Giovanna wasn't on the trolley. After a few seconds, he remembers his car. A trolley heading back to S. Square is waiting for the traffic light to change. The doors are already closed. Jürgen leaps up, runs to the streetcar, and knocks on the door closest to the driver.

The driver acts as though he doesn't see him and stares straight ahead. Jürgen presses furiously on the button that opens the door from the outside. The driver has already thrown the switch that controls that mechanism. In a wild rage, Jürgen pounds on the door with both fists. The light is still red, but the driver refuses to open the door.

An inspector for the city streetcar system grabs hold of Jürgen and tries to calm him down: Be reasonable. The drivers have instructions not to open the doors again once all the passengers have boarded.

But I want to get on, too.

While Jürgen is talking, the streetcar pulls away.

·   ·   ·

Jürgen frees himself and runs back to his car. Out of breath, he squeezes in behind the wheel and steps on the gas. The car roars off and almost hits another car that is trying to pass. Loud honking. Asshole, watch where you're going, Jürgen roars between clenched teeth.

8 9   The woman who runs the pension doesn't understand what he's saying.

With his hands shaking, he writes the name on a piece of paper. Pittui.

Oh, yes, them. They left an hour ago. First the two men came and went up to their rooms. There was a third man with them. A German.

Then everybody came back down again. The two women, the three children—two children—no, there were three. One of the women was carrying a child on her arm. And the two men.

Three men.

Two women, you say. Were there two women?

Was one of them young, a bit on the husky side, long brown hair, wearing slacks and a windbreaker?

Yes, and then there was another one, too, an older, heavier woman wearing black and with a kerchief on her head.

Like the Russian women wear, you know? There were a lot of Russian women working in the factories around here during the war. Or were they Polish?

Jürgen panics. The third man must have been Freddy. Giovanna is moving in with Freddy. He drives through town at fifty miles an hour. He runs a number of red lights, changes lanes erratically, passes cars on the right and left.

The strain sets his nerves jangling.

.   .   .

He knows which building Freddy lives in, but Freddy's name isn't on any of the bells or mailboxes. He rushes up the stairs. None of the doors has "Niebling" on it. What if Freddy has moved?

I was half out of my mind. The only thing I could think of was seeing her right away and convincing her to come back home with me. I couldn't have waited until the next day.

A woman is coming down the stairs.
    Do you know if a Fritz Niebling lives here?
    Up two flights and on the left, the woman says without stopping.
When Jürgen rings the bell, little Massimo opens the door.
    Mamma, Mamma, he calls, and runs back into the apartment.
    Franca comes out of another room.
    She looks tired and worn out.

What you want? Franca asks in an unfriendly tone.
    Is Giovanna here?
    No, gone. They all gone. Freddy, too. To the lawyer.

Now Jürgen loses control of himself completely. He doesn't believe her.
    He roughly shoves her aside. In his mind's eye, he sees Giovanna in bed with Freddy. She is still resisting, but Freddy is forcing her legs apart. Just as he is about to get on top of her, Jürgen bursts into the room. He kicks Freddy's shoulder and knocks him aside.

Jürgen tears open the first door he sees. It's the bathroom. Lavinia is sitting on the toilet. She begins to howl the minute she sees Jürgen. Franca follows him and is suddenly right behind him. Wild-eyed, he pushes her out of his way and runs across the hall.

Sobbing loudly, Giovanna is hiding her face in a pillow. Jürgen yanks open the door on the other side of the hall. A comfortable middle-class living room with two mattresses laid out on the floor. There's some bedding on the dining table.

· · ·

When Jürgen turns around, Franca is standing in the bathroom doorway. She's holding the child on her arm as if trying to protect her from him. All at once he realizes that he is behaving like a savage. His agitation subsides. He is calm again. But he still has to look into the other rooms. He can't help himself. Then, with an apologetic shrug of his shoulders, he slinks past Franca.

Franca looks at him incredulously.

Is he out of his head?

9 0   Jürgen takes up his lookout in an entranceway across the street. It's drizzling lightly outside, and he falls into a reverie in the misty evening. Every so often, a car drives down this small side street. He hears music and voices coming from the corner bar.

After a while, he convinces himself that Freddy, Giovanna, and the Pittuis are sitting in the bar.

As he's just about to open the door of the place, he has a thought: What if they come back while I'm inside?

He opens the door and looks in. He can take in the whole room at a glance. A fat waiter is sitting at a table in front of the bar, playing cards with the only two customers in the place. No music. The waiter looks up briefly.

Jürgen goes back out onto the street and realizes that the music and voices are coming from a third-story apartment.

He is chilled to the bone by the time Giovanna and the others come back.

In the past three hours, he has committed several murders. One time he kills just Freddy, then just Giovanna, then both of them, then himself, too.

Giovanna has been unfaithful to him with Freddy several times. Several times she has come back to him full of remorse.

He can understand how a man can kill his wife or his girl friend.

The desire to kill is intolerably strong sometimes. Anyone who inflicts such emotional pain on someone else cannot be punished severely enough.

Sometimes he considers killing only Freddy, but in such a way that Giovanna doesn't know he is the murderer. Or he'll make the murder look like an accident, or he'll see to it that Freddy simply disappears without a trace.

Freddy stands and waits when he sees Jürgen running toward him across the street. The others keep walking.
Can I come up with you for a moment?
Well, it's pretty late, but come on up.
What's new?
I don't want to talk about it here.

Jürgen feels he has himself reasonably under control.
He has to make a good impression.
Freddy gets a two-liter bottle of red wine from the pantry.
Jürgen comes right to the point: Listen, Freddy. I have an idea.

On Monday, Jürgen will pretend to be Adolf's agent and go get the furniture.
Giovanna is skeptical.
What will the Pittuis do with all that stuff if they don't have an apartment to put it in? Have you thought about that?
Francesco and Patricio nod.

We'll occupy the apartment, Jürgen suggests. Then we'll get my old man to come over, and we won't let him go until he gives it to you in black and white that you can keep the apartment.

Freddy is supportive of Jürgen. His idea is worth considering as a last resort. But for the time being they'll wait and see what the court decision is.

Now Jürgen brings out his heavy artillery.

There's something else I want to talk about, Freddy. It's really why I've come.

I know for a fact that the plant has been sold and will be closed soon.

We have to act immediately.

In Jürgen's fantasy world, Freddy has a whole organization behind him. The minute he has Jürgen's information, all he needs to do is press a button and a well-oiled machine experienced in subversive activity will set to work. The seriousness with which Uncle Hans regards the unknown leafleters suggests how powerful they are.

Every day the papers carry stories about the Communist agents who are trying to infiltrate and undermine every institution in West German society.

Communist agents chip away at the morale of the troops at military bases.

In our schools, the children are subjected to Marxist indoctrination and taught to hate entrepreneurs and the politicians of all the major parties.

The universities have been transformed into training schools for Red cadres.

The Red menace lurks everywhere, even in churches and factories. Uncle Hans Mehlig had a book lying on his desk: *Grass-Roots Activity of Extreme Leftist Groups in the Factory.*

Citizen protests are financed by Pankow and engineered by Moscow. Communist agents have control of the Vatican.

When Adolf was still in good health, he sometimes took Jürgen along to meetings of the local SPD committee in N. The speaker on one occasion was a prominent Hessian SPD politician whom the CDU and the FWG* had branded as a dangerous Leftist. He told his audience that the German Communist Party was the Russian's fifth

*Freie Wählergemeinschaft (Free Voters' Association)—TRANS.

column in the Federal Republic. The German Communists were the greatest existing threat on the domestic front in West Germany today.

Freddy regrets that he has to disappoint Jürgen. Mehlig's statements prove nothing. It's true that Freddy's father is a Communist from way back and presently belongs to the DKP. That's no secret. Mehlig and the government security agencies have known that for ages.

Freddy himself has recently swung back closer to the DKP's position, and he is even considering not running on an independent list again in the coming elections in the plant. He has no organization behind him, and he is not the source of the leaflets that have been distributed in the plant, if that's what Jürgen is driving at.

Jürgen is disappointed. He had thought Freddy was a hero. He's afraid that Giovanna might misunderstand Freddy's remarks. In Sardinia, Jürgen had told her that he was on friendly terms with the leader of the Communist cell at Fahlbusch & Siebert.

But this evening did not remain without consequences. It set off a chain of events that let the case of Fahlbusch & Siebert evolve into the case of Jürgen Schütrumpf. Freddy is determined to call a meeting of the entire work force—even without the approval of the majority in the workers' council, if need be—and finally force the plant's management to show its hand.

Okay, Jürgen, you go on home now. I'll try to get as many workers together as I can early next week. And of course we'll discuss then what Mehlig has told you. All right?

Jürgen has the feeling that he is taking on a grave responsibility.
Sure, Freddy.
He leans down awkwardly to say goodbye to Giovanna.
Take care, Giovanna. And sleep well.
Do you mind if I come back tomorrow?

No, of course not.
The rest of the evening is sheer torture for Jürgen.

No sooner has he left Niebling's apartment than Giovanna sinks into Freddy's arms.

Jürgen goes to bed when he gets home and imagines Giovanna sleeping with Freddy. He pictures every detail of their lovemaking.

As he thinks about this, his own sexual excitement mounts, and he begins to masturbate. He'll suggest to Freddy that they both sleep with Giovanna at the same time. Giovanna is lying on her side with Freddy in front of her and Jürgen in back of her. Their sexual organs touch inside Giovanna. She is a volcano. At the height of her passion, she pushes Freddy away and turns toward Jürgen. Freddy looks on with envy as Giovanna makes love to Jürgen alone.

The weekend passes in a dream state for Jürgen. He spends hours at a time inventing situations in which he distinguishes himself, situations that make him famous overnight, a hero that everyone knows and talks about. He is the bank robber the police have been pursuing in vain for a long time. He is also the mysterious benefactor who has been giving large sums of money to the poor and especially to foreign workers for months now. All the newspapers carry his picture and run stories on him under banner headlines.

During live TV coverage of a state visit in Bonn, he stabs the president of a Fascist military dictatorship to death. While the chancellor and the president of the Federal Republic—the one with the steely smile of a top sergeant, the other with the charm of a custom tailor—shake hands with this dignitary whom the whole world knows to be a criminal and torturer, millions watch on their screens as Jürgen slits the uniformed monster open from stem to stern.

Jürgen plays an especially prominent role in securing the jobs of the workers at Fahlbusch & Siebert. He forces his way into Uncle Hans Mehlig's house one evening and issues an ultimatum. Either Mehlig abandons the plans to close down the plant or Jürgen will blow the whole place up.

A chastened Uncle Hans rescinds his orders. The workers carry

Jürgen through the plant on their shoulders. Giovanna looks up at him with an admiring gaze.

9 1

On Monday morning, half an hour after work has begun, a number of workers crowd into Bachmeier's small office and demand some action from him. Among them are Freddy, the two other dissidents on the workers' council, and some workers from other divisions.

Bach Hein maintains that only the workers' council is authorized to call a general meeting.

Freddy insists that the workers' council meet right now.

His two allies join him in this demand.

Bach Hein tries to put them off. The workers' council is not obliged to call a general meeting unless at least one fourth of the work force requests it. At this point the real trouble begins.

Konrad turns on the loudspeaker system. Everyone in the building can hear what's going on.

Bachmeier doesn't realize what's happening. He doesn't even get suspicious when Freddy's arguments take on the character of a speech. Bachmeier finally notices that the PA system is on when more and more workers stop working and gather around the foreman's office.

There is a scuffle. Bachmeier tries to turn off the loudspeakers.

He angrily accuses the intruders of disturbing the peace in the plant. Since three members of the workers' council have called for a meeting of the council, he says he will discuss the matter with the management.

There is no reason to panic. He will set a time with the management today.

The three dissidents are not satisfied with this. They urge their fellow workers to come along to the administration building right now and express their concern over the rumors that are circulating.

Ten minutes later, the workers form a column and march to the administration building, a flat-roofed, two-story structure built on Industriestrasse in the fifties. The workers want to speak with Director Mehlig.

The office staff and secretaries are standing at the windows. The workers urge them to come outside and support their demands.

Some of them come out, but most of them stay inside the building.

All the doors to the building are locked.

After a while, Bach Hein and the other members of the workers' council make their way through the crowd and are let into the office building. Freddy and the two other dissidents are the only ones who stay outside.

The workers begin to chant. Mehlig! Mehlig!

The chanting becomes more varied. One man calls out a line, then the others join him.

Mehlig! Mehlig! Show your face!

If you don't, we won't leave this place.

Eventually the verses take on a note of ridicule.

Mehlig and Franse!

Come on out and dance!

The office staff watches worriedly as several workers bring up an I-beam and get ready to break down the glass doors and storm the building.

Personnel Manager Franse appears at a window with the workers' council chairman Bachmeier at his side.

Bach Hein begins by asking the three council members who are still outside to come in.

Konrad calls back that they will not negotiate behind closed doors. The directors have to come clean on the issue of closing the plant down, and they have to do it right now and in the presence of all interested workers.

Godfather Franse speaks next.

Director Mehlig is away on business and won't be back until the day after tomorrow.

That's a lie! the workers shout.

Mehlig's company car is parked in front of the building.

Someone yells: Franse! Franse! Bullshit artist!

The chorus repeats this twice, then the voices die down.

Franse says he will inform Director Mehlig of the workers' demands immediately. Sometime in the next few days, the firm's management will answer any and all questions they might have.

Bachmeier asks the men to go back to their work now. They have heard themselves that the management is ready to talk with them. Personnel Manager Franse doesn't know any more than they do. The men have accomplished what they set out to do.

The workers' resistance gradually fades. Although almost all of them are convinced that Mehlig is in the building, they are reluctant to storm it. The discipline that has been drilled into them does its work. Some argue that it doesn't matter whether Mehlig talks with them today or a few days later. It doesn't occur to anyone that the firm will make use of this respite to eliminate the "ringleaders."

The workers stand around in small groups for a while and continue to talk together, first in front of the office building, then back in the shops and at their work stations. After an hour, production is in full swing again.

9 2 When Jürgen arrives for work the next morning, he notices from a distance that a crowd has formed around the factory gate.

He spots some large vehicles on the opposite side of the street. As he comes closer, he sees that they are police cars and paddy wagons. There is even a truck with water cannons mounted on it.

The large entranceway that trucks usually use is blocked off, and there is a police cordon in front of it. The personnel entrance next to the gatehouse is flanked by police, too. The gatekeeper is not seated behind his window as he usually is. He's standing at the entrance, making the opening narrower still. About fifty workers are standing in line in front of the gatehouse.

Why isn't the line moving? somebody asks. Hey, Niebling, get a move on! someone else yells. Jürgen sees Freddy talking to the gatekeeper. As the waiting workers get more restless and impatient, two policemen come up behind Freddy, grab him by the arms, and pull him away.

Freddy doesn't offer any resistance. When the gatekeeper refuses to let Freddy's two friends in, too, the other workers stop going in. They want Freddy and the two other council members to tell them what's going on.

Freddy shows them a letter that the gatekeeper has given him. The workers ask him to read it out loud.

The letter is remarkable for its brevity. It says that the three dissident council members are herewith dismissed without notice.

The reasons given are the unlawful acts of putting the chairman of the workers' council under duress and inciting the work force to riot. The workers' council has approved the firing of the three agitators.

Jürgen is worked up. He feels he has to do something. I had the feeling that I could make up for what my father had done to that Sardinian family. I thought that if I could take part in something at that moment that would help the workers and, even more important to me, that would get Freddy and his friends their jobs back again, I would finally have done something I could be proud of. I had gotten to the point where I felt I hadn't done anything worthwhile in my whole life. I wanted to do something.

Jürgen suggests some form of retaliation.

No one will be allowed to enter the plant unless Freddy and the other two are rehired. Together with some other workers, Jürgen forms a picket line. Several men who are not interested in the discussion and want to go inside are prevented from entering.

The police don't interfere, but the buzzing and humming of their walkie-talkies indicates that the commander of the detail is getting a bit edgy.

Freddy calms the workers down. He doesn't want any clash with the police. Anybody who wants to go into the plant should be allowed to. He and his two friends will go to the labor court right away. There are enough witnesses who can testify that Bach Hein was not threatened and that the workers demonstrated spontaneously and without any urging from him.

Jürgen tries to keep him there.

They have to do something.

We'll storm the gate.

In ten minutes the whole incident is over.

Jürgen is one of the last to go into the plant.

The police stand around looking foolish.

About noon they leave, having stationed only two officers with walkie-talkies at the gate.

Hardly half a normal day's production was reached on this last regular workday at Fahlbusch & Siebert. The debate on whether the workers should strike to force management to rehire the three fired council members goes on all day.

The firm does nothing to stop the discussion. The foremen seem to have been instructed not to provoke the workers. The eight remaining council members discuss questions of a general nature with their co-workers for the first time in years. The major topic is the issue of giving the workers a say in the management of the plant and in the firm's investments.

If the workers had any real voice, we wouldn't have to worry about being done out of our jobs, the men say. The workers have to have the final word on whether a plant will be bought or sold.

.   .   .

Jürgen doesn't take part in these discussions. Silent and almost apathetic, he stands at his machine and works doggedly all day long.

Witnesses later report that he mumbled under his breath. Sometimes he cursed out loud.

His co-workers also testify that he stayed at his machine until quitting time.

Oddly enough, they do not realize until later that he did not change his clothes in the locker room after work.

Months later, Jürgen tries to describe his mental state on that Tuesday, November 19, 1974. I don't know if you've ever had the feeling that you're not yourself. I used to feel that way a lot. You feel that you're made up of a thousand tiny parts that are all different. You feel like a jigsaw puzzle that somebody has put together, but not one single piece in it is really part of you.

Sometimes when I was sitting at a table in a bar, I knew very well that the way I was sitting was not natural to me. I'd picked it up on television somewhere. And that's the way it was with everything. Nothing I did really came from me, not the way I walked or talked, not a single idea I had. I had picked up everything somewhere and adopted it as my own.

When I felt this way, it seemed to me that not even my feelings were mine either.

I had just learned what you were expected to feel in certain situations, how you were supposed to react if certain things happened.

Not even my feelings were genuine.

They were feelings I had picked up from other people.

On that day, I thought I understood that I finally had to do something that came from me. Something I had not picked up from anyone else and that I was not just imitating. Something really out of the ordinary, something that could only be done by me alone.

9 3   At three in the morning, the night watchman hears a huge explosion on the plant grounds.

He runs outside just as a second explosion goes off. He has the impression that some large object is flying up into the dark sky through the roof of the warehouse where the steel is stored.

He runs back into the gatehouse and calls the city fire department. Then he calls up the plant fire marshal, who in turn alerts his squad. All this time, explosions are going off at irregular intervals.

By the time the city fire department and the plant fire squad arrive and station themselves at a safe distance from the warehouse, the building is engulfed in flames. Explosions continue as though there were a grenade launcher somewhere in the blaze. Flames shoot up out of the burning building, which keeps spewing stored metal up through the shattered roof like a volcano.

The commander in charge of the city fire trucks asks the plant marshal: How can something like this happen? What's in that building?

The other man is baffled: It can't happen. It just can't be.

An attempt to extinguish the flames is out of the question. Dangerous shrapnel is coming down in a large radius around the building.

The firemen have to retreat even farther when a sidewall collapses with a great roar and splinters of metal and clumps of other materials come shooting sideways out of the warehouse.

After about forty-five minutes, the barrage is over. Water is sprayed onto the warehouse to cool it down. The radiation-and-pollution-control team goes to work to determine the amounts of harmful gases that have been released into the air.

About four o'clock, Director Mehlig, Bach Hein, and other key officials in the firm arrive.

They are all convinced that this is a case of sophisticated arson.

Someone suggests that the detonations must have been caused by exploding acetylene bottles.

This supports the suspicion of arson, because nothing but materials used in production—steel, sheet metal, pipes, and so on—was stored in that warehouse.

The most likely suspects for an act of sabotage are employees who know the layout of the plant. Mehlig, Franse, and the men from the criminal police and the district attorney's office retire to the administration building.

The minute Mehlig arrives at the scene, a reporter asks him if he sees any connection between the fire and yesterday's incident with the work force.

Mehlig responds emphatically: That's a very real possibility. We know that we have agitators in the plant, and we know every last man jack of them. We'll put an end to their shenanigans. You can depend on that.

Wednesday is Prayer and Penance Day. When the workers come back to work on Thursday, the plant gate is shut. The gatekeepers are handing out leaflets. It will take several days to clean up the rubble and make necessary repairs. As soon as the damage to the plant's stores can be accurately assessed, the workers will be informed by mail when production will resume. The workers are also urged to notify the firm's management or the criminal police if they have any information that might lead to the arrest of the party or parties responsible for the fire.

About eight o'clock, an ancient black Mercedes 300 drives onto the factory grounds. It is Wilhelmine Siebert, that legendary figure, sole heiress to Fahlbusch & Siebert, and still the nominal owner of the firm. Mehlig strides rapidly to the car door and opens it.

The old lady's attorney accompanies her. She is wearing a small black hat. Her loose black dress blows in the wind.

.   .   .

The firm's top officials stand like a cabinet awaiting the arrival of a foreign chief of state. The foremen stand a few steps farther away, somewhat separated from the first group.

Most of the people there have never seen Wilhelmine Siebert before in their lives.

She shakes hands with everyone as if it were not just the first time but also the last.

Later the city fire inspector and the plant fire marshal are introduced to her. She thanks them with that same inimitable expression on her face that she has displayed for decades now whenever she receives the ladies from United Charities and presents them with a check to support their work.

The press photographer at the scene snaps pictures right and left. The next day, the reporter for local news writes a touching article describing how this grand old lady fought back her tears as she surveyed the ruins of the plant it had taken her family three generations to build up.

The editor in chief devotes an editorial to the life and work of the firm's founders and to its eventful history. According to this editorial, one of the last monuments of nineteenth-century free enterprise and middle-class initiative was laid waste in that fateful night. The criminal act of a political madman has wiped out in one blow what had survived the bombing raids of World War II.

The editor of the arts section praises the contributions the Fahlbusches and Dr. Erich Siebert have made to the cultural life of the area. This editor is also the president of the local Goethe Society, which Frau Wilhelmine Siebert, upholding the tradition established by her grandfather, her father, and her husband, has always supported most generously.

The preliminary results of the investigation into the cause of the fire are also available now.

As yet unidentified persons brought several large tubs into the warehouse and filled them with heating oil.

The person or persons then used 250 meters of "C" fire hose belonging to the firm as well as a portable pump to move the oil directly from the plant's storage tanks into the warehouse.

The work of the arsonist or arsonists was made easier by the fact that an old pump the plant fire squad no longer considered reliable enough to use in fire fighting had been left in front of the heating-oil tanks where the plant squad had practiced pumping oil off with it that afternoon.

There are also indications that large amounts of excelsior used for packing and stored in a distant shed were carried to the warehouse and employed as a fuel to create temperatures high enough to ignite the heating oil. Then a forklift was used to transport a number of acetylene tanks from another storage area to the scene of the fire.

The investigators conclude that, depending on the number of people involved, it must have taken several hours to prepare a fire in the metal-storage warehouse that would be hot enough to make the acetylene tanks explode. The site chosen for the fire seems to suggest that the arsonist or arsonists were intent on shutting down production for at least several days, if not for several weeks, by rendering the plant's raw materials unusable.

And indeed this was accomplished, for most of the steel in the warehouse was reduced to scrap metal by the force of the explosions that rocked the building for almost an hour.

Only minor damage was done to the rest of the plant. It's true that there is hardly a windowpane left intact in the shops and other buildings, and the structures immediately adjacent to the warehouse suffered some damage from shrapnel falling on their roofs or being hurled against their walls. If it were not for the problem of replacing the ruined materials, the plant could resume production in a few days.

9 4   The fire at Fahlbusch & Siebert is the talk of the town in N. for the next few days, and even the paper in L. devotes part of its local section to the incident for several days running.

The main point of interest is the search for the arsonist. The paper also discusses the issues of whether there was one person or several involved and why the night watchman claims not to have noticed anything unusual.

He should have heard not only the doors of several storerooms being forced open but also the noise of the portable pump and of the forklift.

Three days after the fire, the paper mentions only in passing that the company has petitioned the Labor Office to permit a mass layoff at the plant and at the same time has asked the state Labor Office to make the permit retroactive to the day the application was submitted. The firm intends to fill only the orders that it has already started work on and that cannot be transferred to another plant.

All other orders and all future orders will be passed on to the Z. Corporation, which bought up the stock of Fahlbusch some time ago and has ample production capacity to handle current orders. There is a possibility that the Z. Corporation will also take on some of Fahlbusch's skilled personnel, assuming that these workers are prepared to move to H.

Public opinion registers this news about the closing of the plant only in passing, too. Exaggerated reports of the damage do their part in convincing people to accept the firm's decision. It wouldn't pay to get the old place back on its feet again.

The few hundred men who used to work at Fahlbusch & Siebert know better, but nobody will listen to them. The union press attacks the firm for using the first excuse that came along.

. . .

A political debate begins to take shape. If it's true that a political madman set the fire, then the case is just one more example proving that acts of political violence do the greatest harm to the cause of the working class.

The *City News*, a weekly paper published by the students at the local technical institute and focusing on things like urban renewal, alternative cultural activities, and current political issues ignored by the official press, raises the question of which is the greater crime: arson that is clearly the product of a disturbed mind or the closing down of a factory that leaves six hundred families without any means of support.

The chief of police consequently designates the staff of the paper an illegal organization. The *City News* is confiscated the day it is published, and a complaint is filed against the editors for publicly advocating criminal acts. The rationale is that the question the *City News* poses contains the implicit suggestion to respond to the closing down of plants with acts of terror.

The police chief's concern is understandable. In 1974, for the first time in postwar history, West Germany is feeling the effects of the grave worldwide crisis of imperialism. The working class is the first to suffer from the increasing number of bankruptcies and factory shutdowns that inevitably result from economic consolidation. Extensive automation reduces the number of available jobs and at the same time increases production and profits.

It is unclear how the workers will react in the long run to the resulting mass unemployment.

On Saturday, three days after the fire, the paper reports that a suspect has been arrested, but it does not publish a photo or mention the suspect's name. The individual in question, the paper goes on to say, is an employee of the firm and has been considered a suspect from the beginning.

Late that afternoon, the local TV station runs a notice from the criminal police, asking for assistance in tracking down the arsonist. A man's picture appears on the screen. The police want to know if anyone saw this man at the scene of the fire on the night in question.

That same evening, two people who have seen the suspect's picture on television report in independently of each other.

They claim that on the night of the fire they saw a young man sitting on the nearly six-foot-high wall that blocks off the plant grounds where the old gate faces on Französische Strasse. The man was sitting with his back against one of the brick pillars that occur at regular intervals along the wall.

The first witness saw the man sitting there at about 2 a.m. and wondered how the fellow got up there. The witness claims he even asked the man what he was doing, but all the man did was to draw one leg up to his chest and remain silent.

The second witness was driving his car along Frankfurter Strasse when the explosions began. He immediately turned in to Französische Strasse, heading for the main entrance to the plant. When he saw the man sitting on the wall, he stopped, got out of his car, and called out: What's going on?

The man looked at him briefly, then disappeared over the wall.

When the police go to the point on the wall that the witnesses described, they find a ladder inside on the plant grounds.

Both witnesses are confronted with a lineup that evening. Most of the men in the lineup are police officers. Both witnesses recognize the man they saw on television. It's the same man who was on the wall. His name is Fritz Niebling, generally known as Freddy.

By this time, Freddy, who was arrested in his apartment Friday at noon, has already had a preliminary hearing. He tries in vain to get in touch with his lawyer. The lawyer can't be reached, the prosecuting attorney M. says. Freddy can always enter an objection to the arrest later, M. adds.

Freddy refuses to make any statements, and the judge signs the arrest warrant. The judge determines there is probable cause on the basis of the report the political police made years ago after searching Freddy's apartment. He also bases his decision on witnesses' statements made about Freddy's behavior at the factory, on Bachmeier's complaint that Freddy had put him under duress, and on Bachmeier's quoting Freddy to the effect that if the plant were closed, he, Freddy, would send the whole place up in flames.

9 5   The first contact Jürgen has with anyone is on Saturday. He has spent the week at home and has only gone into town a couple of times to pick up some things at the store. Edith is not surprised at this. Everyone in N. knows that the fire has temporarily closed the plant down.

And still another factor accounts for Jürgen's staying at home. On the afternoon of Prayer and Penance Day, the day following the fire, Edith wants to go to the bathroom but can't get the door open. Something heavy is pressing against it from the inside.

She and Jürgen manage to open it far enough for Jürgen to squeeze through.

It's Adolf. He is half undressed and covered with his own excrement. He apparently collapsed when he was trying to go to the toilet.

Jürgen and Edith clean him up and put him to bed. He is conscious but very quiet and resigned. Jürgen spends his days sitting in one of the so-called cocktail chairs in the children's room and watching his father sleep in Herbert's bed.

Adolf is restless and tosses around a lot. Edith has put only a long-sleeved undershirt on him and has spread a rubber sheet under the cloth one. Every half hour, Jürgen gets up and dries his father off. Adolf is drenched with sweat. It pours out of his withered skin that has now turned a yellowish brown.

Jürgen gives him fruit juice and stale soda water a few drops at a time. Adolf is very thirsty, but he has trouble swallowing. The doctor says his esophagus is swollen with varicose veins that may rupture at any moment. Also, his edema is worse, and the fluid is affecting his heart.

The doctor urges that Adolf be taken to the hospital immediately. Jürgen is opposed to this idea. Edith is for it. She argues that she can't take time off from work to look after Adolf. Jürgen says that in that case he'll do it. All he asks Edith to do is deliver a letter to Giovanna. In the letter, he apologizes for not having been to see her for so long and asks if she couldn't come to see him now and then.

In the evening, when Jürgen is sitting with his father, he can hear Edith rummaging around in the apartment. She is throwing things out, rearranging furniture, putting Adolf's things away in an old cupboard in the attic, and generally setting the apartment up the way she wants it for her impending widowhood.

Adolf hears her, too.
    See what your mother's doing out there.
    Jürgen reassures him: She's just straightening up a bit.
    Can't she wait until I'm dead? Adolf asks.

Herbert comes home on Friday. He reproaches his mother for acting as if Adolf were already dead. Then, at his father's bedside, he acts like a clergyman. You would have thought it was his job to prepare the old man for death, Jürgen says.
    As if my father didn't know that he was going to die and hadn't been thinking about dying for months now.

When Herbert starts claiming that Adolf always believed in God and had lived a life in accordance with God's will, Jürgen can't stomach the scene anymore. He leaves and waits in the living room.
    Through the open door, he can hear Herbert's attempts to get Adolf to join him in prayer. Herbert recites the Credo in a loud voice.

In recalling this now, Jürgen says: I can't think of anybody less religious than our father was. That was the only area of his life in which he was completely honest. If there was anything he believed in at all, it was nature. After he was taken sick and began sitting in front of his garden shed week after week, he often remarked that humankind had lost all sense of proportion since it had stopped living in accordance with nature.

9 6 Jürgen visits Giovanna after Freddy's picture appears on TV.

She is calm, but the Pittuis are excited and upset. Freddy would never have anything to do with a destructive act like that, they say. He has too much political insight.

You could expect management to destroy means of production, ruin factories, and endanger workingmen's jobs. But any worker has a greater sense of responsibility. He knows the value of goods and of means of production better than any entrepreneur, who no longer needs these things for his survival but only for accumulating more wealth and power.

Giovanna knows that arguments of this kind can't clear Freddy. But she does know for a fact that Freddy is innocent. She can testify that he was with her on that Tuesday night.

Jürgen panics for a moment.

The absurd idea occurs to him that he might be able to win Giovanna back if Freddy stays in prison.

But he immediately rejects the idea. Giovanna won't give him a thought until Freddy is released. He knows her well enough to know that.

The district attorney's office treats Freddy like a political prisoner. He is heavily guarded whenever he is moved from one place to another. The police officers wear bulletproof vests and are armed with machine guns. They transport Freddy in a special armored car with barred windows.

Freddy is kept in strict solitary confinement. He has no contact with other prisoners awaiting trial and is allowed no visitors. His lawyer does not get to see him until Tuesday. On Saturday, the lawyer is refused because Saturday is not a visiting day; and on Monday, the warden tells him he will have to get written permission from the district attorney's office.

On Saturday morning, other searches and arrests are being made all over K. Freddy's two allies on the workers' council are not the only victims. Other favored targets for the police are student communes, the editorial office of the *City News*, and the three Leftist bookstores in town.

The police confiscate a truckload of books, periodicals, leaflets, and manuscripts as evidence. If the press releases from the police department and the reports in the papers can be believed, these searches indicate that a dangerous concentration of potentially violent political criminals with anarchistic and Leftist goals has built up in K. in recent months.

During a protest rally held Saturday evening, several speakers express the suspicion that the police and the district attorney in K., by deliberately overreacting to the fire, want to create in this quiet and provincial city the same atmosphere of hysteria and repression that prevails in the rest of the Federal Republic.

On Tuesday, Freddy's lawyer enters a formal objection to Freddy's arrest. He names Giovanna and the Pittuis as witnesses for the defendant.

He also protests the airing of Freddy's picture on television and declares the statements of the two witnesses who claim to have seen Freddy at the scene of the fire as inadmissible. The streetlight closest to the place where the witnesses say they saw Freddy is twenty meters away. Neither witness could recall what kind of clothes Freddy was wearing.

The officiating judge refuses to release Freddy. He argues that Giovanna has a personal interest in testifying on the accused's behalf because she is living with him in a state comparable to that of marriage.

All that the three Pittuis could testify to was that Freddy had gone to bed at about the same time the two Pittui brothers did. The accused could easily have slipped out of the apartment at some time after that.

Freddy's lawyer contends that, in view of the scantiness of evidence brought against Freddy, continued imprisonment would mean that the accused had to prove his innocence to effect his release. Neither Freddy's behavior in the plant nor his political convictions could be cited as grounds for suspicion that he was the arsonist. Later, long after Freddy's release, the judge will maintain that reasonable cause for suspicion still exists. There is no proof that Niebling did not have some direct or indirect part in setting the fire, particularly since it still seemed probable that more than one party was involved in the crime.

But formal charges are never brought against Freddy.

9 7   A week after the fire, at the time that the judge is refusing to release Freddy, Adolf Schütrumpf's condition becomes even worse.

He spends most of the day in a coma. Only occasionally does he start up and begin to rave. In a loud voice, he defends himself against somebody or other.

When you come right down to it, Jürgen says in the late fall of 1975, all his father did his whole life long was defend himself against something, never knowing whether he was doing the right thing or not. Jürgen keeps coming back to the subject of his father's wasted life. And whose fault is it? The lies. All those lies. Take a word like "peace," for example. All the talk about peace. That we're lucky to live in the time we do and should be grateful. No wars this whole time. At least not in Europe. There have been plenty of wars in other places during this period. Thirty years of peace. As of this spring, we've had peace for thirty years.

But what kind of a peace was it? What good has it done us? I'm not talking about myself now. I mean my father. All he ever did was work like a dog. First came the hard times after the war, then those years of building everything up again. And what good did it do him in the end? All that slave labor? What did he ever get out of life?

All right, so everybody has some moments of happiness. I'm sure he had some, too. But it seems to me a life should amount to more than a few happy moments and just being able to get by—getting enough to eat and reproducing.

Any animal can do that if people don't get in its way. Even cavemen managed that much. I don't see that we've made much progress.

9 8   On Sunday, December 1, 1974, Adolf wakes up during the night. His mind seems to be clear. He is so weak that Jürgen has to hold him up to give him something to drink.

They are alone. Edith is asleep. Herbert is in Schwarzenborn.

Edith works during the day and needs her sleep at night.

For the first time, Adolf admits that he's going to die. Up to now, he has always complained that the doctor is a quack. A decent doctor would be able to get him back on his feet.

Jürgen tries to change the subject.

You've never told me much about your childhood, he says.

After an hour, the old man gradually falls asleep. His speech becomes more and more indistinct and finally turns into mumbling.

Jürgen wakes up at dawn in his own bed. Adolf is drenched with sweat. He is panting, and there is a rattle in his throat. His whole body is convulsing.

Jürgen doesn't know what to do. He calls his mother.

While Edith is phoning the doctor, Adolf begins to choke and cough.

His mouth is wide open. Rhythmic moans rise from his chest.

Suddenly, a thick yellowish-green flood streaked with saliva erupts from his mouth.

The vomit runs down his chin and the sides of his face onto his neck and chest.

Jürgen runs for a bowl and a washcloth. When he comes back, Adolf is spewing blood.

As if transfixed, Jürgen stares at his father's mouth, out of which the insides of the old man's destroyed body seem to be pouring.

By the time Edith comes back from telephoning, it's all over. It looks now as if the mouth under that horrible liquid is moving, as if it wants to speak. The body is completely still.

Edith stands in the doorway with her face turned to one side.

Jürgen wrings out the washcloth and wipes the sweat from Adolf's forehead.

Go get me a big towel and a bucket of warm water, he says.

Edith says, Oh, my God.

9 9   It's eight in the morning when Jürgen goes into police headquarters.

I want to report a crime.

The man at the information desk sends him to the police station in the next entryway.

It takes a while before any of the policemen there get around to seeing what he wants.

I want to report a crime, Jürgen repeats.

What crime?

The fire at Fahlbusch & Siebert in N. I set it.

The officer shows no interest.

Is that so?

Let's see your identity card.

Jürgen hands it over.

The officer slaps it down on the desk in front of him.

Name?

Jürgen Schütrumpf.

Date of birth?

September 17, 1949.

Place of birth?

N.

Occupation?

Plumber.

Address?

17 Frankfurter Strasse.

The policeman nods and hands the card back to him. You can go.

Jürgen tries to protest.

You can go, I said.

Get out of here, or you'll end up in the nuthouse.

Jürgen is nearly beside himself. He insists that he is the arsonist they're looking for.

We're not looking for anybody, the policeman says. Calm down. We already have the arsonist.

I was stunned, Jürgen says. He just refused to listen to me at all. It isn't until that afternoon, when the lawyer G. goes with Jürgen to the district attorney's office to see the assistant DA assigned to the case, that Jürgen can make his statement and get himself arrested.

Even the assistant DA is skeptical. He asks distrustfully why Jürgen is turning himself in. Jürgen says: For love.

Only after a team from the DA's office have visited the plant with Jürgen are they convinced that he knows more details about the laying of the fire than anyone else.

Jürgen shows them the crowbar and other tools he used to break into the various shops and storage sheds. He explains to them in detail how he set the fire. His street clothes are still hanging in his locker, where no one up to this point has been interested enough to look. He leads them into the cellar of the apartment house where the Schütrumpfs live and shows them where he hid his work clothes in an out-of-the-way corner. The clothes smell of heating oil.

All the tools used have Jürgen's fingerprints on them. In the next few days, fingerprints are taken from everyone working in the plant and everyone's alibis checked. The police are able to identify all the fingerprints left by people who might have been accomplices to the crime. But further investigation shows these individuals have airtight alibis.

Despite Jürgen's readiness to confess, Freddy remains in jail. The DA is trying to prove that he was an accomplice to the crime or that he aided and abetted in it.

Not a scrap of supporting evidence for these allegations can be found. After two weeks, Freddy has to be released.

In the weeks following his release, Freddy devotes himself to researching Jürgen's past. By the time Jürgen's trial begins, Freddy has gathered all the major points of Jürgen's history as well as a lot of details, most of which have also been used in this report.

In the trial, the defense's case was based primarily on two arguments.

First, Jürgen acted under psychological compulsion.

Second, the management of Fahlbusch & Siebert had been responsible over a long period of time for creating this compulsion in him.

When the three dissident council members were summarily fired, Jürgen developed a violent hatred for the firm. The management's tactics in keeping the workers in the dark for as long as possible about the closing of the plant, a closing that the plant's directors had known about for months, only increased Jürgen's fury.

Jürgen confirms this interpretation.

The way the firm had hoodwinked the workers had infuriated him. After the three council members had been barred from the plant, he came to the resolve, in the course of that Tuesday, to take vengeance on the firm. The owners should not be allowed to profit from such gross deception of the workers.

He also confirms that he was in an abnormal psychological state. While he was setting up the fire, he acted as if under a relentless compulsion. He can recall every detail as clearly as if he had set the fire many times over. He had thought out every move very carefully.

But at the same time he felt as if his head were encased in concrete. He had had no choice about what he had done.

The court allows that there are extenuating circumstances in Jürgen's case, but it does not find that he was in a state of temporary insanity. Jürgen was in full possession of his faculties as he calmly planned the fire and then carried out his plans. The impending closure of the plant and the firing of the three council members are not relevant and do not constitute any justification for the act.

But it has to be taken into account, the court says, that because of his friendship with Freddy and his close connection with Giovanna Tolu, who, according to her own statements, is a member of a Communist Party, Jürgen was filled with a passionate hatred for the firm of Fahlbusch & Siebert and for the free and democratic political system of the Federal Republic.

He cannot be held responsible for this hatred, which blinded him to the illegal nature of his deed and dulled his sense of right and wrong. He was the unwitting tool of the witnesses Niebling and Tolu, who cannot, however, be prosecuted because there is no evidence against them that the criminal code admits as relevant.

On April 8, 1975, Jürgen is found guilty of arson and other charges and sentenced to two years and eight months in prison.

Apart from some literary details that have been added by the author, this book is based on interviews he conducted with the following individuals: Herbert and Edith Schütrumpf, Dr. Heinz Kreuzhacke ("Bübi"), the house painter Hassenpflug, Frau Pels, Uwe Hühnerfuss, "Käse," Ilse Gutberlet, Erich and Hilde Schindewolf, Hans and Anni Mehlig, Heidrun, Hans and Käthe Kamprath, Heinrich Bachmeier, Fritz Niebling (Freddy), Franca, Francesco, and Patricio Pittui, and Giovanna Tolu.

The Pittui family has returned to Italy and is now living near Parma.

Giovanna Tolu is living in Orgosolo and working as a German teacher in a high school in Nuoro.

The descriptions of living quarters and individuals are based on the author's personal observations.

The author has changed the names of the characters.

Kruspis, March 16, 1976.

A NOTE ABOUT THE TRANSLATORS

Robert and Rita Kimber are free
on an old farm in western Mai
Although their training was
Literature, the nature of th
them beyond these fields. I
and poetry, they have don
history, art history, sci
sailing, and have rais
sheep. The Kimbers'
and *Laws of the Gam*
will also be publis

A NOTE ABOUT THE AUTHOR

Peter O. Chotjewitz was born in 1934 in Berlin, and until now has written primarily for the theater, for radio, and in short story form. He lives in Kruspis, in Hesse, where he also practices law.

A NOTE ON THE TYPE

The text of this book was set in Olympus, a film version
of Trump Mediaeval. Designed by Professor Georg Trump
in the mid-1940s, Trump Mediaeval was cut and cast by
the C. E. Weber Typefoundry of Stuttgart, West Germany.
The roman letterforms are based on classical prototypes,
but Professor Trump has imbued them with his own un-
mistakable style. The italic letterforms, unlike those of
so many other typefaces, are closely related to their roman
counterparts. The result is a truly contemporary type,
notable for both its legibility and versatility.

Composed by Superior Printing,
Champaign, Illinois.
Printed and bound by American Book–Stratford Press,
Saddle Brook, New Jersey.

Book design by Judith Henry